LIVING LAND

LIVING LAND

THE GARDENS OF BLASEN LANDSCAPE ARCHITECTURE

TEXT BY HAZEL WHITE • FOREWORD BY CATHERINE WAGNER • PHOTOGRAPHY BY MARION BRENNER

ORO
EDITIONS

Published by
ORO *editions*
Publishers of Architecture, Art, and Design
Gordon Goff: Publisher
www.oroeditions.com
info@oroeditions.com

Copyright © 2013 by ORO *editions*
ISBN: 978-1-935935-46-9
10 9 8 7 6 5 4 3 2 1 First edition

Edited by: Eric Blasen and Silvina Martierena Blasen
Book Design: Pablo Mandel / Circular Studio

Color Separations and Printing: ORO Group Ltd.
Printed in China.

This book was printed and bound using a variety of sustainable manufacturing processes and materials including soy-based inks, acqueous-based varnish, VOC- and formaldehyde-free glues, and phthalate-free laminations. The text is printed using offset sheetfed lithographic printing process in (book specific) color on 157gsm premium matte art paper with an off-line gloss acqueous spot varnish applied to all photographs. ORO *editions* makes a continuous effort to minimize the overall carbon footprint of its publications. As part of this goal, ORO *editions*, in association with Global ReLeaf, arranges to plant trees to replace those used in the manufacturing of the paper produced for its books. Global ReLeaf is an international campaign run by American Forests, one of the world's oldest nonprofit conservation organizations. Global ReLeaf is American Forests' education and action program that helps individuals, organizations, agencies, and corporations improve the local and global environment by planting and caring for trees.

Library of Congress data:

For information on our distribution, please visit our website
www.oroeditions.com

Contents

Foreword

by Catherine Wagner, Artist
Professor of Art, Mills College

*A true poet does not bother to be poetical, much in the
same way a gardener does not scent his roses.*
JEAN COCTEAU

The gardens of Blasen Landscape Architecture operate like poems, not calling attention to themselves, but guiding our relationship to the worlds they've created. Eric and Silvina's gardens are made real by structured interventions in the existing land. Their designs give form to new vistas allowing for the possibilities of undiscovered views. They frame the natural surroundings, revealing to us new microcosms of these worlds. In this manner, the Blasens' gardens do not disrupt the urban or natural environment, but allow us to better situate ourselves and invite us to consider the philosophical possibilities of the act of seeing.

Their designs transcend traditional categories within the field of landscape architecture in an embrace of pluralism, drawing from the natural world, the visual arts, minimalism, and modern architecture.

Their gardens offer an evolving experience throughout the four seasons, providing reflections of their own careful observation of change in the season and interaction of the cultivated with the natural. Their inspired designs of walls, meadows, circulating water systems, both lush and spare planting plans create sublime gardens for both observation and respite.

The current inhabitants and future visitors to their gardens will delight in coexisting with these spaces that continue to grow and change, embracing the life cycle.

Living Land offers us an intimate journey through these environments.

A way of seeing, a way of making

Interview by Hazel White

Eric Blasen and Silvina Martierena Blasen have created gardens on all kinds of topography, from mountain, foothill, and city slopes to the ocean shore. Land, plants, and design are the passions they share, and art, and most of all, connecting clients to their land.

HAZEL   Thinking about interviewing you, I remembered the first garden of yours I saw. "Who built this garden?" I asked urgently, and then I sought you out, to stand in more of your gardens. I think of that moment in that first garden as an experience of beauty, the way Harvard Professor of Aesthetics Elaine Scarry describes beauty—an experience that requires, mandates even, below the level of thought, a journey to replicate the experience. For almost twenty years, you have been making gardens together, in every kind of site from mountain tops to the ocean shore, and, in writing the text for this book, I have now seen many of them. You create special places. Can you say what you do? What is it exactly that you set out to make? Do you call it a garden or a landscape?

SILVINA   We call it a garden. It's a place that makes you feel at ease, a place where you can rest, observe, just be, enamored with trees and flowers but also with the surroundings that make you comfortable—you have a good chair, a nice patio, you have shade, you have sun, all these elements that give you options on how to spend your time outdoors. Contact with nature is very healing. People seek that.

HAZEL What is this place you set out to make?

ERIC It's very personal and sort of private actually. We're creating something completely custom, completely for the client. We are making the walls, that is, green walls, really making the space. As Silvina said, we think of the space seasonally, and even at different hours, where would I want to sit in the sun or the shade, where is it cool, and where's the view. We think about all these things, to give a client all the possibilities, and then there's a dialogue with them, and then the ideas get refined on how they are going to live there. We have a dialogue back and forth, making drawings to do the refining, to come up with the best solution for the client and the site. A garden is marrying those two.

HAZEL A customized relationship between the clients and their land?

ERIC Yes, definitely.

SILVINA And the way they live. What is the way they live; that is what we try to find out, so we can cater to that.

ERIC Some people entertain a lot, some are private, and some are both.

HAZEL Silvina, you are admired for your use of native plantings in contemporary landscapes. I know you have long relationships with the great nurseries in California and have an extensive knowledge of plants. What do you like about natives?

SILVINA Natives give the garden a sense of belonging to that place, so it's not completely foreign to it. But the biggest issue is the low water use; water use is the most important thing in California today. We arrived in California in 1989, when a drought had been going on for four years, and it lasted three more years. I couldn't have imagined anything like that before. Natives make so much sense. They are beautiful and adapted to this climate. One of my favorite plants is manzanita. You see those trunks, and why not use that plant! I just find them beautiful. And most people's thinking has changed about natives. When I began, it was very difficult to sell the natives concept because people thought they looked scruffy and weedy. But nowadays, I design with natives in many areas, wherever they'll thrive.

HAZEL Stewardship of the land is a passion for many homeowners right now. One form this has taken is an interest in edibles gardens. How do you design the plantings in these gardens?

SILVINA Usually I look at the herbs, the perennials, and also the seasonal plants, and I create different areas for those, and of course, the long-term plantings such as the fruit trees and the grapevines. I separate them. And then by season, by what you plant in the spring and what in the fall or summer. My edibles gardens are client—or gardener—oriented. I ask the client what do you want to eat. It's all about that too.

HAZEL At the Light Touch on the Land garden [PAGE 50], the edible plant list was quite extraordinary.

SILVINA It was long because the client has space to grow a lot of things, and then she extended it to many Chinese vegetables.

HAZEL That was a steep site. You built a beautiful edibles garden on steep rocky land, I think?

SILVINA We did. We mixed the soil with compost. First, we test the soil; we want to make sure it is rich in minerals and has the correct pH and no toxic elements. After that you can improve it; if it's very clay, you break it down; if it's very rocky, you add water-retaining elements.

ERIC The trees are down the hill, so they don't shade the other planting beds. We are thinking about sun orientation too; we always make a solar study. There's a high value to an edibles garden; it connects you to the land. It engages people to be part of that, get their hands dirty planting, and then nurture the garden. When you think about Japanese gardens, their design, the stepping stone paths, for example, everything makes you have to stop and look. Slowing down is a good thing.

SILVINA Some clients use the garden as a tool to teach their children. You start a pumpkin, and in five days you have a shoot and in ten days a giant. You plant it in the right place, give it some water, and it gets big. That grows on you; you want that. You garden because of that, not just because the fruits of the labor are edible and you take them indoors.

HAZEL That's striking—in the 21st century people want to grow their own food to teach their children and grandchildren. Spaces for children to play are common in your gardens. Is it often part of clients' wish lists, to educate their children about land?

SILVINA Our clients put a high value on their gardens. It comes from that. For them, it's really important. If they don't value their land that way, they don't call us: they put in a hedge and a lawn and call it a day.

HAZEL Eric, how has sustainability become a part of your design practice?

ERIC Sustainable systems are set up now, and they are more affordable. It's automatic. The city requires you to do it, for one thing. It's part of the process as we go into the project. Before it wasn't; it was an add-on, now it's just part of it.

HAZEL You mean balancing cut and fill if you shape the land, so you don't need to bring in soil or take it away?

ERIC That, and also when to use permeable and impermeable surfaces, and not having water run off the property, water absorption, not destroying the natural features of a site, having a light touch on the land, avoiding materials that are toxic, limiting the energy use, using recycled materials, all these things.

HAZEL What is your favorite material?

ERIC I like our native oak trees; they are sculptural and have such grand scale. Even though Silvina does most of the planting design, I do some. Among building materials, I like concrete; it's a great material in walls and paving. And I definitely like steel; we've used it a lot, in gates, trellis, and walls. I like to mix materials, such as wood, stone, and earth.

HAZEL   The material richness in your work is interesting. I think I saw it in the Woodland Clearing garden.

ERIC   Yes. There's natural stone there and cut stone, interesting colors and textures; I create compositions with cut stone and crushed stone and honed stone and metal. I'm always cognizant of not doing too much. It's easier to do too many things. The hard thing is restraint, to pull it back; then it's more powerful, more calming too as you go into a space. You want it to be sophisticated. How one material attaches to another material, how and where transitions take place: I am constantly looking at those things, obsessing about those things, coming back into the office and telling somebody, Oh I just thought about something we should do…Some people can walk through a space and not really look at it. I think we're cursed almost from that, because we always look, we see all of it.

HAZEL   And you are working with the architecture and existing trees. You are not timid about scale in your work, I think.

ERIC   No, not at all. It is very important to get it right. To create proportional relationships between gardens and architecture.

SILVINA   It's hard to narrow your palette to a few materials that will do all the jobs you need done.

HAZEL   Isn't it the editing that creates the quality that you often mention—seamlessness? It's an aesthetic?

SILVINA   I think so.

ERIC   Yes, editing a design takes restraint and attention to detail. It is important to understand how the architecture engages the landscape, through sensitive grading design, material selection, and planting scale, so it all comes together to a seamless composition.

HAZEL   I think you look for a calming composition—it's as if you leave space for the clients to notice the breeze or the weather changing, or things happening in the space. You have to edit hugely to allow the feeling of the space to occur there? Is that what you do?

ERIC   Yes.

HAZEL   Otherwise, it's distracting of the nature of the space?

SILVINA   Yes, where there's a lot of things, I feel uneasy. I don't want to stay. We try to avoid ornamentation at all costs.

ERIC   When we do traditional work, it definitely gets more ornamental.

SILVINA   Because it follows what's there.

ERIC   We'd rather be true to what is.

HAZEL   You were a geography major, Eric. Later, you studied art and entered the long process of becoming a landscape architect, and also designed furniture, I think?

ERIC   My father was an artist; I got inspired. He also made and designed furniture. When we started our office in landscape architecture, we didn't have much money and we didn't have any furniture so we were making our own furniture. It started there, a need for us. But it was also, for me, a need to experiment with materials. I wanted to go to the metal shop, the wood shop; I've always been intrigued by how things are made. My explorations into that dovetailed well into landscape architecture; it's all building.

HAZEL   Why did you choose landscape architecture? I know you both have a huge interest in architecture.

ERIC   I like the diversity of the work. I like being outside. And that I can build at many different scales. As a geographer, you are studying the world. My view went from a macro to a more focused and more micro view. I was a generalist when I was young, interested in science, people, and art. I was unfocused. Then I worked as a planner/geographer in an architecture firm, and we made maps and plans, but it was conceptual and nothing got built; all bubble diagrams. It was a multidiscipline firm, and I saw what the landscape architects did, and I knew I wanted to do that. It was about building and it took into account

many complex issues, which suits me well.

HAZEL   Through all your work, I see a beautiful simplicity of line and form. Does that go back to your interest in natural landscape?

ERIC   Yes, and interest in art. Those two. Art inspired me to look in a different way at the world, the built landscape and the natural landscape. It opened my eyes. A way of seeing is a big part of being a good landscape architect.

HAZEL   Are your favorite artists sculptors?

ERIC   They are. What we do is three-dimensional, and an installation in space, if you will. I definitely like Richard Serra and Donald Judd. And Robert Smithson, the different scale, and the light. James Turrell, he's all about light. Those artists inspire me a lot. And Andy Goldsworthy, he's delicate, where he takes things, and makes you think of the natural landscape in a different way.

HAZEL   I think you once mentioned Olafur Eliasson's site-specific work?

SILVINA   Yes, definitely, we like his work, the way he uses natural forces to activate his art—water, light, wind.

ERIC   The Christo umbrellas in southern California transformed my thinking. Everything, I thought afterwards, it's all about composition. You could think an umbrella composition was random, and then, when looking at it closely, it was so beautiful, so balanced, with the light. It was a moving experience for me.

HAZEL   I had driven that way many times and hadn't noticed the details of the topography. After seeing the Christo umbrellas, I always saw the little canyon opening onto the valley floor there, for example. Is that what you mean? Not just the composition of the umbrellas but the ...

ERIC   Yes, exactly, the umbrellas and the natural landscape, how they engage each other. You look at it again, you look at the flat plane, how the road and the hills and sky connect to it.

HAZEL   That's what's special about your gardens, I think: an animation between elemental things and the space. Suddenly, you see how light comes beautifully through those trees, across this clear space, because you have thought about those things.

SILVINA   Yes, that's definitely a way to look at it. And it happens through the seasons, how the light moves, and shadows become longer, what gets activated in late afternoon sun, say, in midsummer on a north side, things that only happen for a couple of months a year.

HAZEL   Silvina, is there any part of Eric's work that you are interested in yourself?

SILVINA   Yes, his designs. I like what he does, the way he designs things. He has a very minimalist approach.

We share that. I do large masses of plants, and I repeat plants over and over, which gives continuity with the design and goes well with the scale of the buildings and the site.

ERIC   You have to be really sensitive to do this work—I hope the sensitivity shows in the work—and one of the things we do really well together is help each other. It's reassuring to get another opinion. Although we talk about work out of the office, I don't look at it as a grind. On the weekend, we usually take a walk up in the hills with the dog, we hike a lot, and we talk about the landscape, the topography and plants, that massing, say, only a few species.

HAZEL   At the Beach Headlands garden, Silvina, you said you like to work with what is already growing on the site. The number of plants that can be grown here in northern California is vast, so why do you like to work with what already is, what does it teach you?

SILVINA   It makes the garden belong to that place. Then, it's from there. When we work nationally, outside of California, the first thing we do is study the plant palette there, research the flora of the area. There has to be some connection with them there.

HAZEL   Your clients often become your friends. As you revisit the gardens you've made, what most interests you about what you created for your clients?

SILVINA   How the garden has aged.

ERIC   Yes; everything is bigger and filled in and healthy. We want to make people happy, that's important to us.

HAZEL   Do you want to say anything more about what a garden is or what garden making is? It's a form of human making, alongside architecture, but it springs from a desire to articulate something deeply cared about, do you think?

SILVINA & ERIC   Yes.

ERIC   I think it's not just the space in itself. We are creating a refuge for our clients, a place for them to be calm and think, and then the stewardship component, of doing the right thing with the land, weaving design into natural systems. When I look at garden making—I don't want to call it our art form—it's our passion about design; it's our medium.

HAZEL   I think I understand why your gardens feel so beautiful. Thank you.

PROJECTS

01 Urban Play

LOCATION San Francisco, California
ARCHITECT Gemmill Design

Viewed from above, this tiny Tadao Ando–inspired garden is eye candy—a lively composition of folding planes that extend the minimalist architecture and contemporary interior design out onto the land. Down below, inside the garden, is a children's realm, animated by play.

From their unused, steeply pitched, weed-filled plot on a San Francisco hill, the clients wanted the Blasens to make "a safe place for the children to feel bold." Now their young twin girls chase up and down the tipping topography, roll, slide, climb the rope, dig, and plant. They create games, tea parties, and camp-outs with sand, water, twigs, leaves, and flowers, their days shaped in a web of relationship with the land.

Upstairs, family members and guests move casually between indoors and outdoors along the Italian granite flooring that runs over the threshold. As they descend toward the garden, down the flat-bar steel stairways, the garden switches from dynamic view to deeply felt place. At the farthest point, at the end of the garden sheltered by walls colored to match the house, they can look back up to where they were through the swaying palm fronds of the neighbor's tree.

The garden is made private by towering step-up double scrims of pittosporum, two varieties (one variegated, one green), one behind the other. Beneath them, other plantings spill over the retaining walls, in a carefully chosen, restricted palette of purple, white, and yellow. The project is environmentally sustainable: the rubber paving at the base of the slide and the metal gate and railings at the entrance to the service area were all made of recycled material. The grading design balanced cut and fill. Bioretention drainage was installed. The plantings are drought tolerant and irrigated, only as necessary, by drip irrigation.

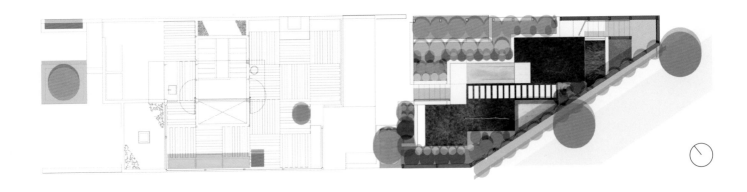

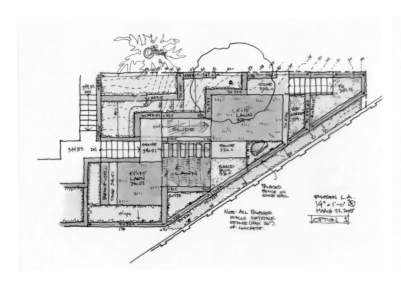

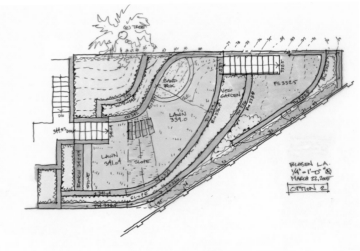

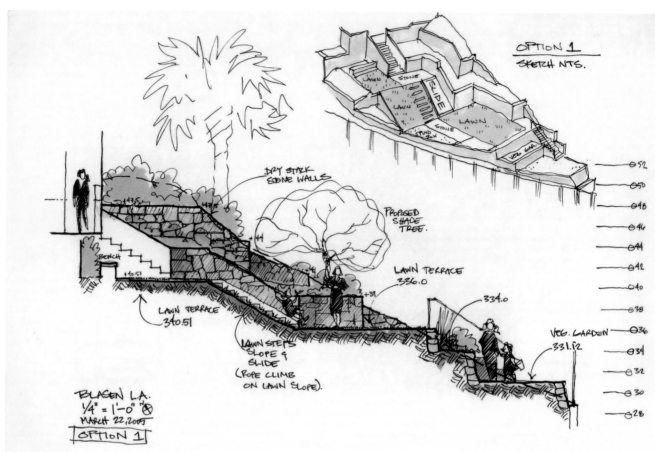

OPTION 1
SKETCH NTS.

DRY STACK
STONE WALLS

PROPOSED SHADE
TREE.

LAWN TERRACE
336.0

334.0

BENCH

LAWN TERRACE
340.51

LAWN STEPS
SLOPE &
SLIDE
(ROPE CLIMB
ON LAWN SLOPE).

VEG. GARDEN
331.12

BLASEN L.A.
1/4" = 1'-0"
MARCH 22, 2005

OPTION 1

Θ52
Θ50
Θ48
Θ46
Θ44
Θ42
Θ40
Θ38
Θ36
Θ34
Θ32
Θ30
Θ28

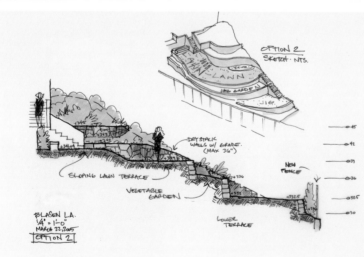

OPTION 2
SKETCH · NTS.

DRY STACK
WALLS W/ GRADE.
(MAX 36")

NEW
FENCE

SLOPING LAWN TERRACE

VEGETABLE
GARDEN

LOWER
TERRACE

BLASEN L.A.
1/4" = 1'-0"
MARCH 22, 2005

OPTION 2

Θ45
Θ42
Θ39
Θ36
Θ32.5
Θ30

02 Beach Headlands

LOCATION Stinson Beach, California
ARCHITECT Pfau Long Architecture

The ocean sometimes pounds so strongly along the beach, the vibration runs through this garden well back on the shore. Sand flies in the wind, burying washed-up trunks of eucalyptus in the dunes. Sharks chart the sparkling water. Close-in, on calm days, locals dive to pry abalone off the rocks.

Kim and her three teenage children used to come out to their 1/3-acre property here only on weekends, walking about 100 yards from the garden gate to swim and surf. But then, after the remodel of the home, and the new garden by the Blasens, they decided to live here, enveloped in the salty air and the rhythm of the waves.

"For seven months of the year, we use the courtyard more than any of the indoor rooms," says Kim. "It's a kitchen, a living room, and a hallway. We cross the courtyard to the bedrooms rather than take the indoor hallway." Working at her desk just off the courtyard, she looks out at the tall white plumes of the Peruvian feather grass. "They move constantly," she says, "They make me think of music—and that sequence in 'American Beauty' of the bag floating in the air." Many evenings, her teenagers and their friends sit around a bonfire at the fire pit. "It's a throwback to a more innocent time," she laughs.

Bringing in sand for sand dunes, the Blasens planted native grasses in them, including native deer grass, and myoporum trees and passionflower vines, which grow like weeds along the coast. "We make more of what already is, so the garden belongs where it is," says Silvina. She pruned up the existing myoporum, watered and fed the existing rhamnus trees, and propagated the yellow bulbine, a succulent perennial native to South Africa, that was already growing here.

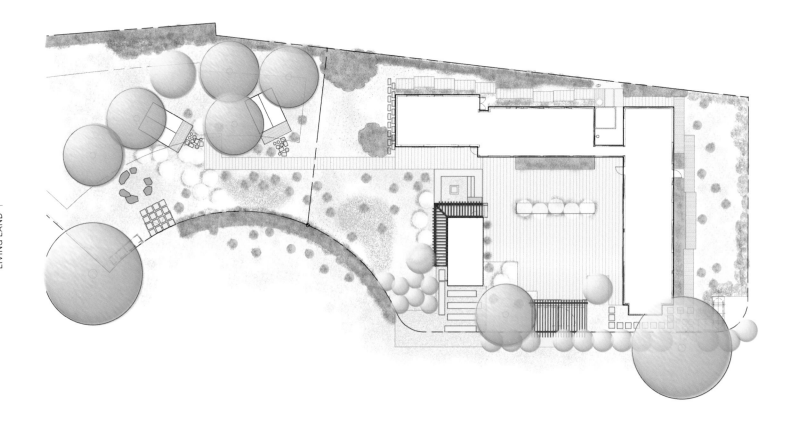

03 Oak Weave

LOCATION California
ARCHITECT Jim Jennings Architecture

On neglected land, in a forest of weedy invasive eucalyptus trees, under which nothing will grow, a couple of old oaks had held their ground. The architect sited the home in the shelter of them, the eucalyptus trees were cleared, and Eric and Silvina planted more full-size oaks to restore a natural habitat.

At the house entrance, the landscape architecture twins reverently and lyrically with the architecture. Playing off the architect's bump-out of mahogany wood in the stucco wall, Eric composed a bump-out of a clipped hedge in a Corten steel planter. He designed the courtyard walls to match the color of the architecture; and through the archway, where the floor switches to a red sandstone (note the Richard Serra steel sculpture that bumps up from the paving), the grid design plays on the grid of the architect's concrete snap-tie walls. The collaboration is seamless—architecture and outdoor space, one.

Similarly, the plantings are strong and simple next to the architecture. "The intention was not to distract from the architecture or the art," says Silvina, "so nothing overly pretty, and nothing that framed the art, just strong large plantings." For example, in the entrance court, a long mahogany trellis holds one variety of rose and is underplanted simply with rosemary; the minimalist pond—the water flows out of a brimming trough in the courtyard wall and under the paving in a geometric "stream" to the centrally placed pond—features one plant, corkscrew rush.

Below the house, the gravel paths, edged with rocks from the site, thread around the hillside in lines that are reverent to nature. Under the oaks grow swaths of drought-tolerant native manzanita, ceanothus, and western sword ferns. Many specimen trees and shrubs with richly textured foliage, stems, or bark and stunning flowers provide cutting material for floral arrangements indoors. Because of the solid serpentine rock, each planting hole was jackhammered out and given its own drainage channel. In the shady, deeply sheltered areas far from the house are secret-feeling places for the grandchildren to play.

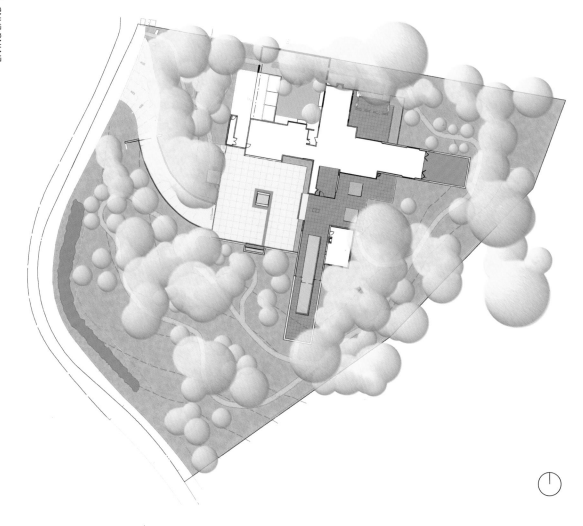

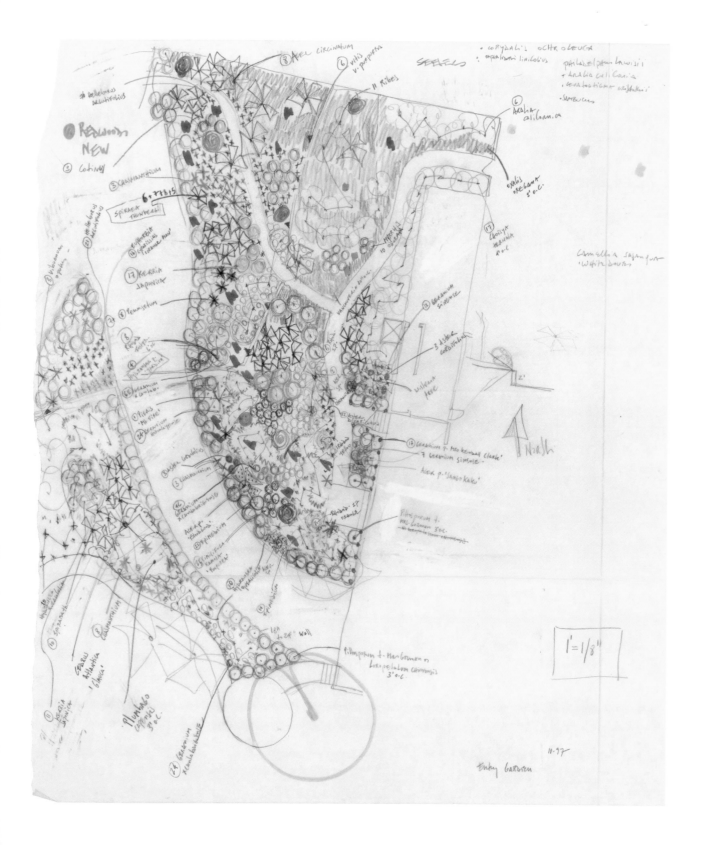

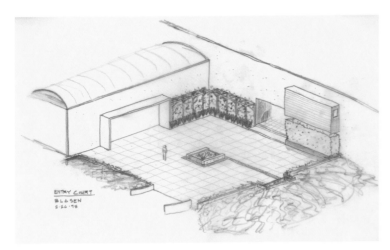

ENTRY COURT.
BLASEN
2.26.98

FOUNTAIN
BLASEN
2.26.98

04 Light Touch on the Land

LOCATION Calistoga, California
ARCHITECT Eliot Lee, Steven Harris Architects, and Eun Sun Chun

Before any house was here, you might have walked over this land on a ridge high above the Napa Valley, stepped between scrub oaks, stirred up a fragrance of sage, and found shelter in a hollow to watch a rare spotted owl soar above the windy hilltop. And so you could now. Listening to client Tatwina Lee speak of her childhood summers with her grandmother in a cabin in the coastal mountains, the Blasens set about establishing pristine encounters with this land she loved.

They urged the building contractor to protect the landscape during construction. They took each piece of excavated limestone rock and used it for a step, boulder, or the compacted gravel-earth paths that they made narrow and meandering as if worn out of the vegetation by the wild turkeys and occasional mountain lion that also inhabit this land. They took care of the native plants, gathered seeds and cuttings and propagated them, and respected the way the water flowed after rains.

Tatwina, who comes here with her husband most weekends, practices qigong on a mound facing west, swims under a wide sky, tends vegetables in a garden tucked out of view, walks along a trail to sleep in a cabin that floods with moonlight. "It's very special that this place is so close to what I wanted, even if I didn't know what I wanted at the time we started," she told the *New York Times*, "I could move here full-time in a heartbeat."

The first time Silvina saw this land she noted "the plants that want to be here," she says. When it became a construction site, aggressive weeds took over, but with careful tending she brought the wild plants back. Where the moisture seeped in late winter and early spring, she sowed poppies. She planted ceanothus and manzanita, knitting together mounds of blue-greens and mahogany bark to restore the original feeling of the place. "The land talks to you. I try to help it out," she says.

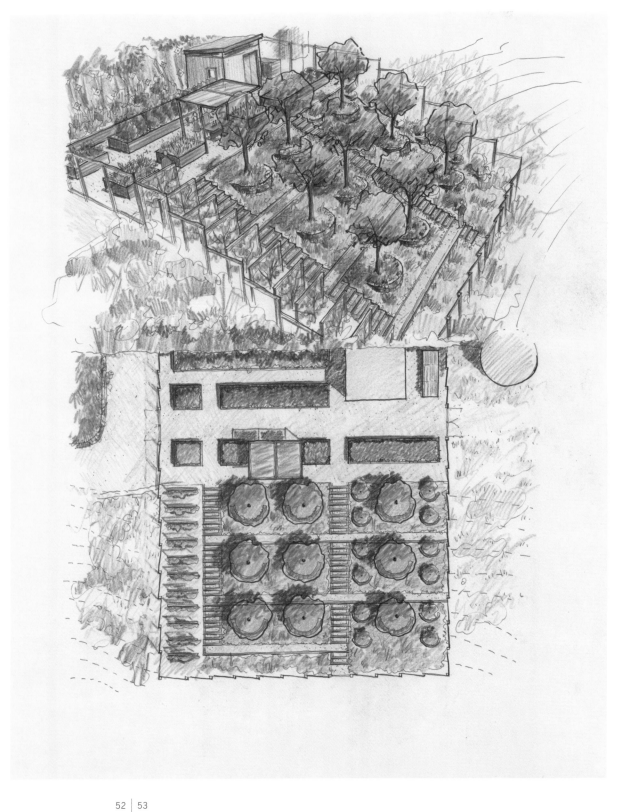

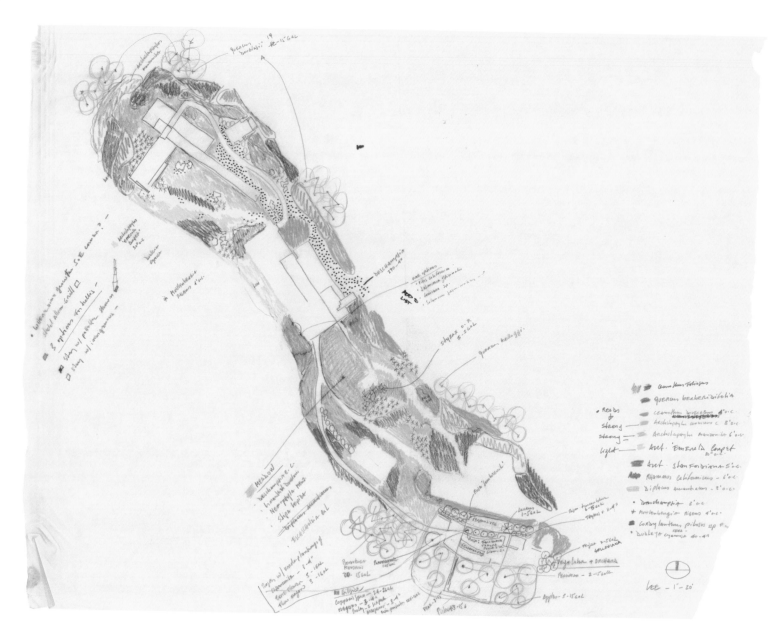

05 Meadow Park

LOCATION California
ARCHITECT Atelier Ugo Sap

At the roadside, the entrance to this property stands out only in its subtle modernist interpretation of a post-and-rail fence. Entering, under a well-preserved old oak tree, one passes through gates and over a bridge, plain and beautifully designed.

Only decades ago, when nature was valued differently, on a large private estate, one usually saw imposing architecture extended into grand allées of lawn and fountains. This 21st-century private estate reflects an opposite, thoroughly contemporary philosophy.

Emerging from the shade of the trees at the creek, one arrives into a bright meadow that flows up the hill to the skyline. The residence is tucked into the knoll of the hill, only partially visible behind trees. Since there's no immediate requirement to greet it, one can enjoy a slow, relaxed ride up around the meadow.

It is this seven-acre meadow that proclaims the grandness of the property, as much as the contemporary and late-20th-century sculpture that is sited on its fringe, where it meets the forest. For more than five years, the meadow has been slowly restored to its native condition, free of the invasive foreign grasses that have spoiled California meadows. It has been seeded and reseeded with fine native grasses, and mowed so that light reaches the slower-growing native grasses and they have a chance to establish. The tough invasive grasses, which sprout from the existing seed bank in the soil and often grow quickly and tall, have been pulled by hand, every single one. When the invasives are entirely depleted, native wildflowers will be sown among the native grasses.

On the meadow edge, the driveway advances up the hill in the play of sunlight and shadows created by occasional groves of oaks. The trees veil the house from view until a final rise brings one onto the auto court—and to a panoramic view over the house roof of the meadow, its enclosing forest, and the western hills.

Steps between rows of ginkgo trees and textural plantings lead down to a sheltered fireside patio by the front door. On the other side of the house, a lawn under London plane trees abuts a lap pool, with an infinity edge over the meadow. Here, and at the house sides, plantings including gaura and manzanita spill from the garden into natural groups on the hillside.

On another part of the property, off the main driveway and out of sight, is a guesthouse with a pool. Here, too, is a small organic farmstead. One enters through an informal orchard of fig, mulberry, apricot, citrus, peach, and cherry trees. Beehives are sited nearby. Two large trellis houses with small-mesh screens keep flowers and vegetables and berries out of the reach of wildlife. Outdoors grow hardier vegetables,

kiwifruit vines, and pomegranate and filbert trees. Long tables are set up for parties.

An earthen path leads off toward the boundary of the property, through large drifts of native shrubs, into a vast natural bowl under redwood trees. Ferns grow throughout the bowl; native orchids will be seeded among them.

What's not in view is the estate infrastructure, which also reveals a contemporary philosophy: runoff from the meadow enters a biolfiltration system before returning to the natural aquifer. There's a large solar panel array, and a geothermal unit for off-grid heating and cooling.

"The challenge," recalls Silvina, "was to protect what was already here." Fifteen trees already on the property were lifted and boxed during construction of the house and estate, and then later replanted. Hundreds of mature trees were also brought in and grown in boxes until planting could begin. Only the kitchen garden/farm and the small garden close to the main house require regular watering. The largest part of the estate is intended to be irrigation-free, as any highly prized natural land would be.

06 Garden Above

LOCATION San Francisco, California
ARCHITECT Pfau Long Architecture

The clients' home is a beautifully crafted, rambling shingle but with no space to be conventionally rustic. It occupies a lot on a San Francisco street rather than a rolling slope to the New England shore. From two small roof decks, the Blasens designed exquisitely crafted contemporary outdoor living spaces, including the furniture (Eric's first career interest was furniture design). As important as the elegance is the experience of nature in its minimalist essence: a world different from the indoors, a sequence of sunrise and twilight and seasons, each approaching storm and returning sunshine tuning the everyday experience of the family who live here.

On the main roof deck, Eric set out "to make the space big with the least number of design moves." Sustainably harvested Ipe hardwood decking floats on a river-pebble base, asymmetrically, on either side of the limestone pad that runs out from the living room—a series of spaces with unhindered traverses. At one end of the area, a bench pops up out of the deck, playfully and yet with the least disturbance of the space. At the opposite end, to anchor the longest possible view within the area, is a water feature. Between the two, almost transparent, sits a dining table.

On the narrow upstairs roof deck, the richly toned palette of materials is configured vertically: tall, narrow fountain and planters, a stainless steel trellis and round table. From the deck rail, one can see the main roof deck below, its asymmetrical pattern reflecting the asymmetry in the shingle architecture, the simplicity and timelessness, and lack of over-ornamentation and waste, characteristic of the Japanese influence on shingle style.

The plants require very little water, fertilizer, or maintenance. Silicone-bronze planters hold Corokia cotoneaster. Hollywood junipers twist skyward out of tall planters, providing immediate screening of the neighbors' windows. Because the plants are not numerous, each is encountered as a form, a presence alive in the outdoors and a reminder of nature—when fog drifts in through the Golden Gate Bridge, it hangs around the junipers just as it does in the cypress on the cliffs.

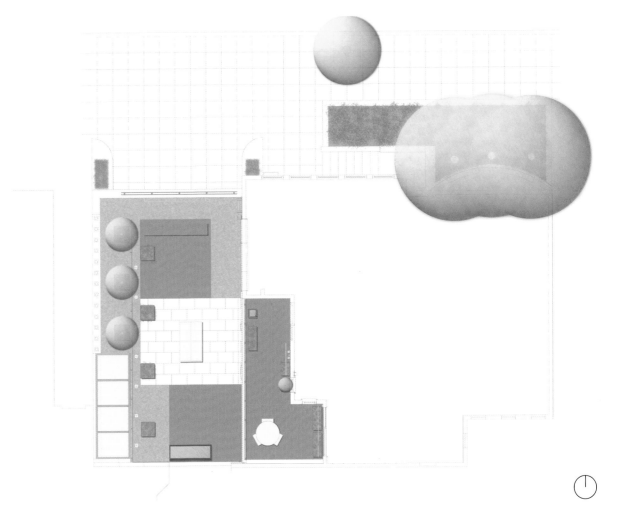

9.21.01 OPTION 1

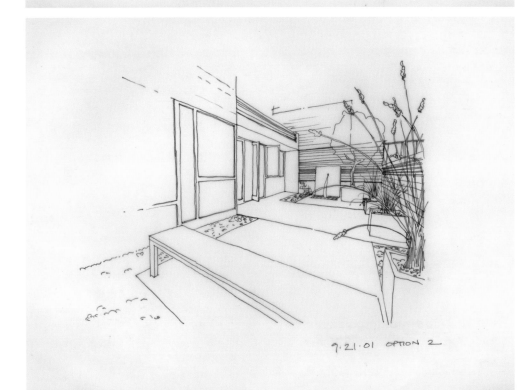

9.21.01 OPTION 2

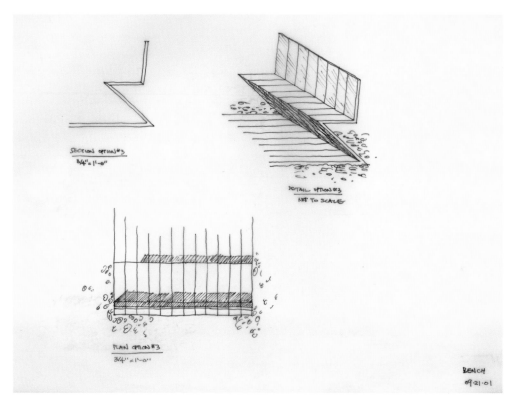

SECTION OPTION #3
3/4" = 1'-0"

DETAIL OPTION #3
NOT TO SCALE

PLAN OPTION #3
3/4" = 1'-0"

BENCH
09·21·01

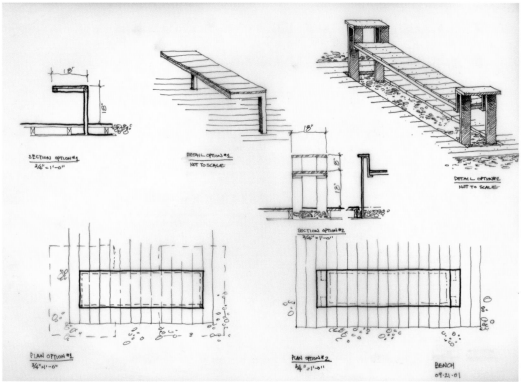

SECTION OPTION #1
3/4" = 1'-0"

DETAIL OPTION #1
NOT TO SCALE

SECTION OPTION #2
3/4" = 1'-0"

DETAIL OPTION #2
NOT TO SCALE

PLAN OPTION #1
3/4" = 1'-0"

PLAN OPTION #2
3/4" = 1'-0"

BENCH
09·21·01

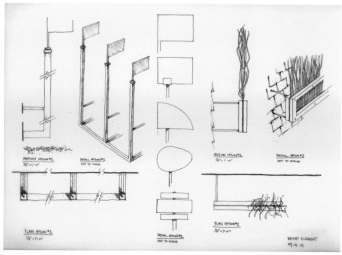

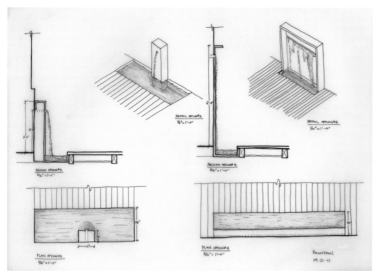

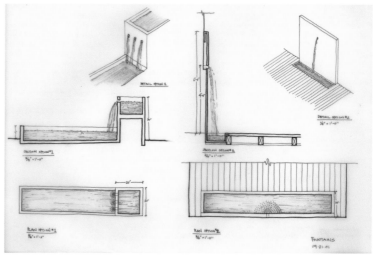

07 Terrace Connections

LOCATION Oakland, California
ARCHITECT Regan Bice Architects, Fischer Architecture

The garden lies along a finger of land inside a hairpin bend in the Oakland hills next to a popular trailhead into a canyon. The family who lives here wanted privacy and also to preserve the connection to public open space. Working with them, the Blasens designed a garden that is sheltered, private where necessary, and yet also porous to the natural landscape and activity outside it.

Coming uphill, hikers pass the entrance garden and an olive grove with lavenders—both entirely open to viewing. At the hairpin corner, the fence is still open, though lush small trees screen the guesthouse rooms. On the uphill perimeter, a hedge is loose enough to allow for a little peeking and low enough to keep open the view from the road to the canyon and the San Francisco Bay. Each of the five steel-and-recycled-redwood gates leading into the garden, designed by Eric, is also partially open in construction.

Inside, a formerly very steep, eroding, and unused slope is now a sheltered clearing where family members lap-swim, play with the dog, eat, and nap in the sunshine. The pool, designed by the architects, is made private by a three-foot-high wall on the outside edge, though the family enjoys overhearing hikers appreciating the garden from the road below. Seating at the hearth provides a deep peaceful shelter against the hill. Steps lead up the terraces to fruit trees and also vegetables that can be grilled over the fire. At the top of the garden, the light at the end of the day flows pink through the canyon eucalyptus, and an aerial steel walkway gives a view over the Bay.

Native plantings, such as manzanita, California fuchsia, and California lilac, draw birds and butterflies into the garden from the canyon. Red-leafed cercis settle the original red-brick entrance path into the land; the generous Mediterranean-style house rests comfortably among the olives and lavender.

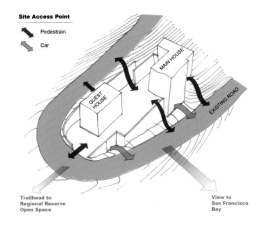

Site Access Point

→ Pedestrain
→ Car

GUEST HOUSE

MAIN HOUSE

EXISTING ROAD

Trailhead to
Regional Reserve
Open Space

View to
San Francisco
Bay

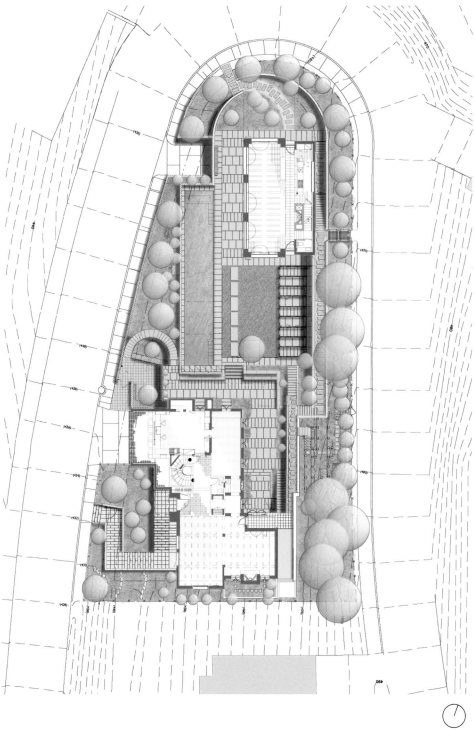

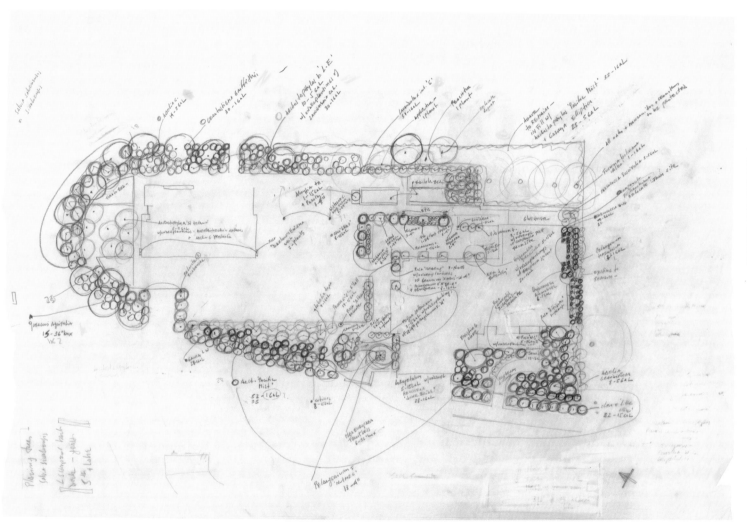

08 Oak Park

LOCATION California
ARCHITECT Atelier Ugo Sap

The allée of linden trees at the entrance to this large, romantically planted property is a paradise for honeybees in June. Arriving, you see them busy in the flowering treetops and working in and out of the roses and cranesbills. They are ranging far from their hives at the "farm."

The owners of and visitors to this contemporary residential park, with its majestic old oaks, are offered many experiences and excursions into the land. At the main house, the largest of the terraces provides a long view of the center of the park: through a drift of tall meadow grasses, stairs roll down across shaped sweeps of mowed lawn under oak trees, toward the pool and pool house, and the view extends to the wooded slope in the distance.

Walking the land, one gains intimacy with it. The meadow grass, native red fescue 'Molate', is silky fine; every zither of air combs the tips across the hillside, before quickening the movement of the leaves of the oaks. At the poolside, white petals from streaming wisteria on the arbor dust the furniture arranged around the fireplace. The pool includes a lap swim area, exercise bar, Baja water bench, and spa.

A bridge that comes into view crosses a creek and reveals an aqueduct; much restoration work has been done to ensure native trout can travel through this stretch of the creek to spawn upstream. Water draining off the hillside to the creek passes through a swale that is planted with shrubs and trees to absorb some of the water flow and prevent erosion. Irrigation water from the lawns collects in a tank and recycles into the planting beds.

Beyond the creek, a tennis court backed by redwoods comes into view, as well as a basketball hoop and a bocce ball court behind a Chilean myrtle hedge. Then the kitchen garden/farm, with a fountain near the beehives to provide water for the bees so they don't drink from the pool. Pollen- and nectar-rich plants such as lavender, herbs, and michaelmas daisies feed the bees in summer and fall, and the bees pollinate the apple, pear, cherry, and apricot trees when they are in flower in spring. Honeysuckle and elderberry shrubs attract birds; plants such as verbenas and salvias make a butterfly habitat. Rows of vegetables and honey in the hives supply the kitchen. But here, one is farthest from thoughts of the elegant house. The view is peaceful, full of scent and the calls of birds.

Walking along the boundary now, one more destination completes the tour: a full-size labyrinth, where the color of the edge stones and gravel path blend with the bark of the shading redwood trees.

Silvina saved many of the existing trees and shrubs on the property, including dogwoods, magnolias, and hydrangeas. The owners asked for flowers, so she added more species of flowering hydrangeas, lots of cranesbills and roses, including Peachy Creeper, her favorite, a shrub rose that is soft yellow-orange fading to cream. Many annuals, such as lobelia, pack seasonal color—usually just one color—among the green shrubs. Some of the shrubs, such as native huckleberry, have edible fruit—"I love to have fruit everywhere," she says.

The plantings are contemporary romantic: lush, very green, full of movement and softness and scent; many flowers, but in each area the same color tone, so not at all fussy, and nothing rigid or too straight. The bank of wild grasses next to the house is a particular triumph, always remarked on: "It's calming," Silvina says.

09 Woodland Clearing

LOCATION Atherton, California
ARCHITECT Aidlin Darling Design

Topping the list of what the owners needed was play space for their children. The tall home—reminiscent of a Cape Cod farmhouse but with a contemporary California twist—was new and needed to be settled into the landscape and shaded from hot summer sun. The owners wanted roses and an edibles garden. The soil was clay and the water table high, so drainage would be a problem.

The Blasens listened, asked questions, brainstormed with one another. Later, they threaded each request artfully through the layers of construction and design work that also organized the beauty of the architecture and the most exhilarating prospects of the site. Each client wish was granted, and in the process the large flat site surrounded by towering redwoods and old trees on neighbors' properties, including a magnificent oak, became an expression of horizontal and vertical, a woodland clearing.

At the entrance off the leafy street, camphor and magnolia trees spread high over the car court, which doubles as a basketball area. Planted paperbark maples and a linden tree at the house connect it to the existing "woodland." A stone wall—of chopped stone, both rural and somewhat formal, exactly matching the elegance and rusticity of the home—extends the architecture into the landscape, settling it there. At the rear of the

house, a planted grove of ginkgo trees at one edge steps up to the architecture, shading indoor rooms in summer and filling them with sunlight in winter; the opposite edge, following the lines of the home, steps out into the clearing, again formal and breaking with formal.

From the verticality of these trees, and the nested patio with roses below them, extends a specially drained play field—straight back to the property line, the plantings and fireside seating near the pool kept very low and the guesthouse, ping-pong table and trampoline sited to one side in order not to interrupt the grand light-filled sweep.

Fruit trees and edibles beds and more roses sit on the sunny side of the house. At the rear of the property are massings of low-maintenance plants such as *Verbena bonariensis* that attract butterflies.

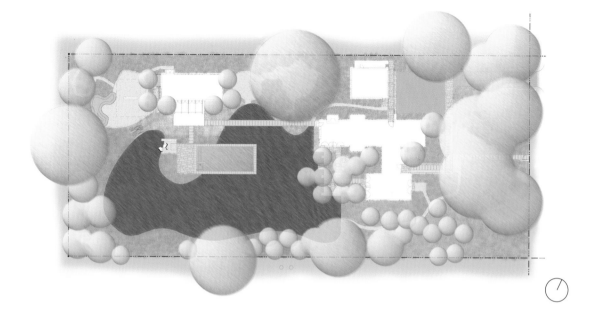

10 Open Range

LOCATION Healdsburg, California
ARCHITECT Atelier Ugo Sap

A home and landscape sited and designed exquisitely strike up a melody of right relationships. One feels a rhythm of built line to natural topography and to one's own movements. As if recognizing a forgotten dance, alertness runs through the body. "It's beautiful," we find ourselves saying, again and again.

This landscape was drawn on paper, and then on site visits, the Blasens were allowed to move the blocks of architecture, still also on paper, to create the greatest fluency of space and feeling in the outdoors. Arriving off the road, you hear the crunch of crushed gravel as you park under trees. A choreographed "entrance sequence," as Eric describes it, takes you down "a very soft grade change" to the house, which was carefully nested into a plateau in the wooded hills. Between pairs of shallow steps are broad landings, which turn and slow down your motion, and communicate the expansive open rhythm of this place.

Later, exploring out of the house, lawn steps drop you graciously to the pool terrace; beyond it, the land drops again gently into plantings. The phrasing of this landscape is also played in the low walls. The eye, and then the feet, follows them out away from the house, picks up on the wall fragments, trusts the continuity running the length and breadth of the space. The plantings extend the lines sometimes: a hedge of

Japanese euonymus runs from the house alongside a patio and beyond it into oak woodland; rows of ginkgo trees march across a glass hallway between two sections of the house. The plantings also make broad horizontals; grouping single species in masses, Silvina creates floating planes at different heights. The plants are top performers, a signature of her planting style.

"They look well in bud, when they flower, and when they seed," she explains; "they are tough, they bloom over a long season, and, except for the lawn, the landscape is drought tolerant, even most of the roses."

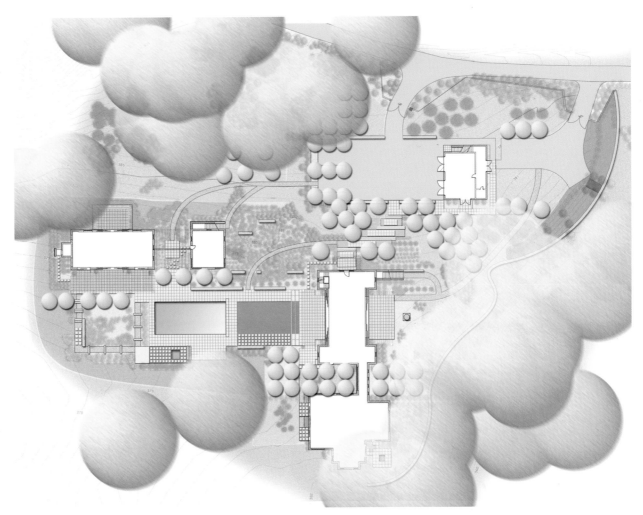

11

Ocean Frame

LOCATION Big Sur, California
ARCHITECT Sagan Piechota Architecture
STONE MASON Edwin Hamilton Stoneworks

This 70-acre property drops steeply from a mountain above California's scenic Highway 1 near Big Sur to the ocean edge. Arriving, one meets nature in thrilling scale—west, the Pacific Ocean; east, the mountain range; and north and south, Big Sur's famously rugged ocean cliffs and sandy coves. The home sits below the road, out of sight; the garden, a complex "composing of the hillside," flows below it toward the water.

From a cobblestone patio at the house, the land rolls downhill gently in designed planes to the bottom terrace, where long stone benches hold the edge of a sculpted lawn. The shaping responds to the arc of the ocean; the scale is masterful, embracing the wild expanses and providing comfort within them.

At the first terrace, a wall glides out of the topography, sweeps around an oak, and is anchored at the edge of the hill by a boulder. Under the oak, beside the wall, sit a burled wood table and bench for peaceful dining.

The next descent is via curving steps bordered by a thick stone wall and purple fountain grasses shifting in the breeze. Arriving at the middle terrace, one can seek the quiet of the horizontal axis, along grass terraces in the shelter of magnificent walls crafted by the stonemason from the rock on the site. At the bottom lawn, reached by more curving steps, these in

a lavender field, the waves can be heard on the rocks below and the sun sets into the curved horizon. Looking back, one sees the house nestled in the land folds, the garden, irrigated by the natural drainage water, slipping into the view of the mountains.

"This garden is about movement," says Silvina. "The ocean is full of motion, and the sea birds are flying through the spaces." Surrounded by such large scale, the plantings needed to be big gestures too: a hillside of billowing lavender, lots of a few local species—Carmel creeper, white Monterey lilac, dune buckwheat, Point Sal purple sage.

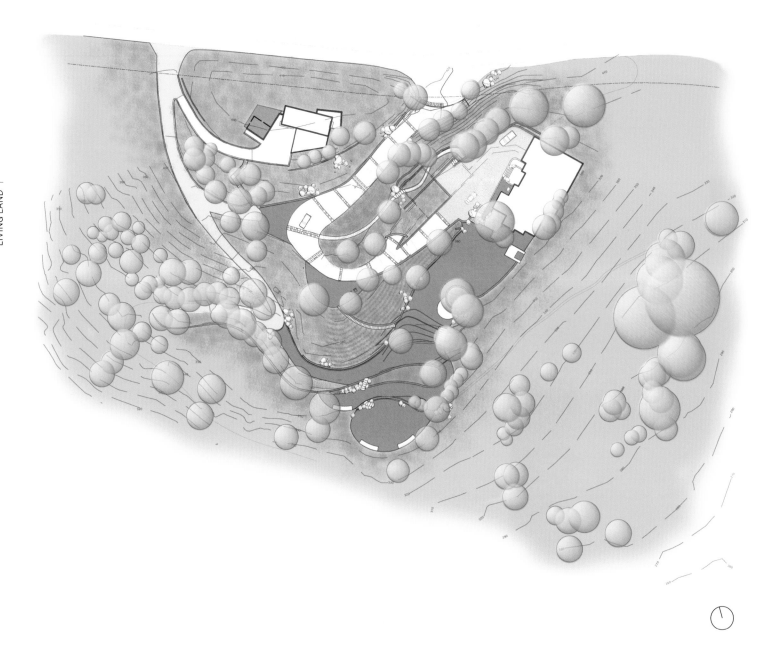

Lexicon

As Eric Blasen and Silvina Martierena Blasen have gone on passionately about their work, they have etched out a vocabulary of design that is custom to them. It reveals both a vibrant aesthetic at play in the present and the influence of their backgrounds, personalities, deep thinking, and pleasure in richly textured, durable construction materials and plants.

Beauty. It's an unspoken goal. It should not be something you go for straight on, or else you get pretty, without depth, instead of beautiful. Beauty is a matter of the proportion and scale of the architecture and trees, the color and texture of the plantings and the consequence of many, many decisions, and they all must be right. It isn't a conceptual matter; it must all feel right. To say a garden is beautiful is an expression of emotion. Not one thing can be off. EB

California culture. I think people are more experimental here. We can be more daring. EB

Chopped stone. It's blocky, has some randomness in the irregular edges, but stacks tight, has a dry laid look if you rake the joints back. Overall effect is great: crisp with some softness. The rust tones in chopped Elk Mountain stone work well with bluestone paths (page 125). EB

Cohesiveness. When you don't know who's designed what, the architect or the landscape architect, we love that. Collaborating with the architect, there's a chance for us to do the work in a way that when you walk on to a finished site, it all feels at ease, unforced, as if it had always been there. EB

Color. If the color is wrong, everything's wrong; it shocks you. We look at color in great detail, the color of the hard materials as well as the soft ones. And in plants, it is not only the color of the leaf and flower, it is all the parts of plants through the seasons, from the new spring leaf to fall coloring, the stems and trunks, the bud color when it opens and when it ages, and fruit color. Texture changes colors; light touches color differently during the day and in different seasons. Color creates a state of mind, and one's humor or disposition. SB

Compound curves. A series of connected arcs, to edge planting beds, for example, feels more continuous, flows better, and is more dynamic than a pure arc. EB

Construction. A construction process can be stressful for clients, so we aim for a very different experience, one that is professional and enjoyable. EB

Lexicon photographs by Silvina Martierena Blasen, except Marion Brenner where indicated.

Ease. We aspire to design spaces that put people at ease with themselves. SB

Editing. The design process is about editing. First, we visit a site and decide what stays and what goes. Then we make adjustments to emphasize particular features of the site. The third step is the creation of something new, but appropriate; we want to create thoughtful and timeless designs, distilled to their essence. Our work is about purity—and emotion, and the pleasures of everyday living. EB

First visit. When I first visit a site, I see the vegetation and slope, the views, the weeds, the native and nonnative plants. The type of vegetation gives clues to the soils and sun exposure. I look for the most valuable elements on the site, what to preserve at all costs. We absorb the site, find a way to read the language of it. In essence, we make more of what already is, so it belongs there. SB

Green. People say to me, we want color. I tease them, I say green is a color. It's my favorite color. If I had to stick with one plant, only one, it would be boxwood—all green, takes sun and shade, you can do any shape, and you can keep it small. And I love its texture. Although,

on one big job, just when I was finishing the last part, the architect said, I hate boxwood, it smells like pee, and the client said take them out. Not everyone thinks the same way. But everything looks good with green, any color. My second favorite color would be blue, a dark blue. SB

Hardworking plants. I have a few plants I call my hardworkers—they are there to do a job, and they do well in sun, and they do well in shade and with water and without, in wind, mistreatment, no fertilization. For example, I use pittosporums, which are great performers, when I have to make sure that an ugly view is never open again, and grasses and Point Sal salvia to hold firm an eroding hillside. SB

Influences. Early on, before we started our own firm, Garrett Eckbo invited us to his home in Berkeley; I remember he stressed the importance of doing good work and designing a variety of projects. Dan Kiley, who I worked with, was an influence, too, in terms of his very nice modernist approach to the landscape. My friend Pablo Pardo, a lighting designer, was very encouraging to me when I was a furniture designer. In the early 1990s, we were part of a design salon called SF3, which met monthly; I learned a lot about how things are made. EB

Landforms. I like topography. I grew up near the Cascade mountain range, so I really like mountains. The scale of them. I feel lucky to live in sight of Mount Tamalpais; the redwood forests thick with ferns, the native grass meadows and open vistas—its diversity inspires me. EB

Landscape architecture. We are designing with living things and natural systems, responding to climate and the change of light and weather and to the soil. What we build evolves over time, becomes a representative of time, and in a way, reveals the process of time to the people who live there. It's a form of art maybe, in the way it helps people to see things, but it's not conceptual; it's a real living place, for people's enjoyment. EB

Lightness. We go for the least. We don't like overdoneness. SB

Mattress vine. A wonderful plant that I use by itself. It's not a good neighbor; it will smother other plants. SB

Music. Like music, the garden sets a mood, and there's a rhythm as you walk through. Entering the Beach Headlands garden, page 35, for example, is an experience like crescendo: You step onto the threshold beneath the arbor, turn, touch a long handle. Suddenly, a whole section of cedar fence spins open, revealing the expansive courtyard. Surprised, you turn, and step up onto it. Then, there's a slowing down, soft plantings, places to sit. But sooner or later, you take the boardwalk through the grasses toward the sounds of the waves, which draws you toward another crescendo: turning to go back to the house—a sudden majestic view of the coastal headlands, gold in the setting sun, with home nestled at the foot of them. It had been at your back all along. EB

New. We pride ourselves on each garden being very different. Our design strategy is always a reflection on the particular site, where it is, what the client is doing and wants to do there, what the site challenges and best features are. EB

North-facing places. The most difficult thing is how to plant on a north face, because it's completely in shade most of the year, except in the middle of summer when it's in full sun at midday, the hottest time. There aren't many plants that take that. Some good ones are boxwoods, several varieties of sedges, dwarf plumbago, and coffeeberries. SB

Ordinary things. Some of the best designs come out of reflecting on and refining the vernacular, refining ordinary things. A compost bin, for example, that's about ease of use: with slide-out slatted walls and a concrete floor for easy turning of the compost, and a hinged lid that's opens easily and is pleasant to the touch. EB

Our own garden. We live in a California oak woodland, across from Mount Tamalpais. Those large oaks are precious, sculptural in form, providing shade in summer, shelter, and beauty. Priceless, because they took so many years to grow. We have redwoods in the wet area of the garden, towering symbols. The garden is about selection—different garden spaces for different times of the day during the seasons, morning sun, afternoon shade, intimate enclosed places, the sunset view. We have afternoon lunch parties, outdoor dinners, and a bocce ball court that we use. We grow food and have an orchard. The physical activity teaches you how things grow and work. It's a place to enjoy by myself, with family, and with friends. And a place to experiment. It connects me back to the land and an awareness of time. EB

Peruvian feather grass (Jarava ichu). It produces the softest tall white plumes in spring through summer.

In California, it will regrow and may bloom again if cut back and fertilized by midsummer. SB

Plant advocate. I call myself a gardener. When we start a new garden, I come from the gardening place: what are we saving, what are we moving. I'm the plant advocate. I'm obsessed with plants. I go to all the nurseries, I go everywhere, to find treasures. SB

Plants. Plants matter. They are the soft element that brings warmth and life to gardens. Plants touch people. The new California licensing exam for landscape architects no longer requires plant identification skills; that's fundamentally wrong. People expect landscape architects to know plants. SB

Poetic spaces. My goal is to achieve a purity of form combined with a density of emotion. EB.

Red. Red makes things pop. You put one red flower over there, and the whole composition lifts. I am not afraid of it, but some people are. When I first moved to California in 1989, red was like a bad word. It was impossible to plant red things. When we did the Oak Weave project, in 1998, the client wanted red. That was the first time. SB

Restraint. We are not trying to always make a statement. This is where there's a moment, say, and then this is where you pull back. EB

Scale. More and more, I use fewer species and greater quantities of them. If you use a lot of species in a large space, it looks out of scale. SB

Seamless. At the Beach Headlands garden, page 33, we designed the fence and arbor with cedar planks to match the house and garage siding; we extended the existing Trex decking in the courtyard to make a boardwalk around the house and out into the garden. The color of the fire pit concrete was matched to the sand and the plumes of the grasses, even the color of the tree trunks was considered. EB

Seeing. My father was an artist and graphic illustrator and a dreamer. He taught me how to see. On Sunday drives in the VW bug, when I was growing up in Oregon, he would point out the beauty of boulders in the river and the composition of a native stand of Douglas firs. EB

Silicon bronze. Used thin for containers, it's lightweight, ages well, and has seamless edges. EB

Silvina's inspiration list. The poetics of Luis Barragán, the designs of Isamu Noguchi, the color schemes of Gertrude Jekyll, the audacity and freedom of Christopher Lloyd, and the plant knowledge of Beth Chatto and Graham Stuart Thomas.

Site. We read the important elements of a site, what rules there, what the essence is of the place. We refine it, then create compositions that use its visual cues. SB

Site investigation. We investigate all facets of a site: topography, sun/shade, views, privacy screening, drainage, sounds, wind, water, city codes, existing trees and plants, fire protection, historical significance. Then we synthesize it with the needs of the client, and then that's what drives the design. It's site-driven and custom design. EB

Specimen plants. More often now, we plant gardens that have large specimen plants, so that clients have instant screening or an instant giant tree next to the house that brings the scale of the architecture down. That is a dream come true in many ways. We used to finish a garden, and everything was so small and the house looked so big, and you had to wait. SB

Tadao Ando. His clean, smooth, concrete walls and efficient use of space were a design inspiration for the Urban Play garden (page 26). We created snap-tie concrete walls, colored to match the smooth stucco of the house, to retain the terraces and planting beds, visually extending the architecture into the garden. Italian granite, the flooring indoors, is continued outdoors in the steps that float down the slope, and in the seat of a bench that cantilevers from a concrete wall. EB

Tree protection. I look at everything through the eyes of the plant. A big part of what I do during construction is to protect the trees. I stop the workers from putting heavy toolboxes and piles of wood under the tree canopies and compacting the soil there. Or storing plants under the native oaks and watering them. SB

Weeding. Weeding is gardening. It is like watering, one of the most important things. You have to be on top of it for the first few years after planting. In our own garden, I weed a lot in early spring. I take an area, do a piece at a time. It's a meditative task; it frees my mind as I focus on taking out the whole root of each weed. Weeding builds up patience, which I think is a great virtue. And gardens need care. They disappear if you don't care for them. SB

Plants

URBAN PLAY

Shrubs
Cassinia leptophylla – silver heather
Lantana montevidensis 'Alba' – trailing lantana
Olea europaea 'Little Ollie' – dwarf olive
Pittosporum tenuifolium – kohuhu
Pittosporum tenuifolium 'Marjorie Channon' – variegated kohuhu
Rosa 'Charlotte' – yellow rose
Rosa 'Gourmet Popcorn' – white rose
Spiraea thunbergii 'Mt Fuji' – baby's breath spiraea
Vines
Jasminum officinale 'Grandiflorus' – poet's jasmine
Jasminum polyanthum – pink jasmine
Rosa 'Sombreuil' – white rose
Perennials
Campanula poscharskyana – Serbian bellflower
Teucrium scorodonia 'Crispum' – wood sage
Trachelium caeruleum – blue throatwort

BEACH HEADLANDS

Trees
Cupressus macrocarpa – Monterey cypress
Myoporum laetum – lollypot tree
Thuja 'Emerald Green' – emerald green arborvitae
Shrubs and Vines
Cassinia leucophylla – silver heather
Passiflora 'Constance Elliot' – white passion flower
Rosa 'Sombreuil' – rose
Perennials and Grasses
Jarava (Stipa) ichu – Peruvian feather grass
Muhlenbergia rigens – deer grass
Otatea acuminata aztecorum – Mexican weeping bamboo
Pelargonium tomentosum – mint scented geranium

OAK WEAVE

Acer circinatum – vine maple
Acer palmatum 'Bloodgood' – Japanese maple
Acer palmatum 'Sango Kaku' – Japanese maple
Cedrus atlantica 'Glauca' – blue cedar
Corylus avellana 'Contorta' – contorted hazelnut
Eriobotrya japonica – loquat
Fagus sylvatica 'Tricolor' – tricolor beech
Ficus carica – edible fig
Lagerstroemia indica – crape myrtle
Magnolia grandiflora 'St Mary' – southern magnolia
Magnolia stellata 'Royal Star' – star magnolia
Michelia doltsopa – sweet michelia
Oxydendron arboreum – sourwood
Parrotia persica 'Vanessa' – Persian ironwood
Persimmon 'Fuyu' – persimmon
Prunus persica – peach
Quercus agrifolia – coast live oak
Sequoia sempervirens 'Aptos Blue' – coastal redwood
Shrubs
Ceanthus 'Dark Star' – small leaf mountain lilac
Corylus cornuta californica – California hazelnut
Feijoa sellowiana – pineapple guava
Grevillea 'Superb' – grevillea
Hydrangea quercifolia – oak leaf hydrangea
Hypericum androsaemum 'Albury Purple' – St John's Wort
Isoplexis canariensis – Canary Island foxglove
Kerria japonica – kerria
Leptospermum horizontalis – horizontal tea shrub
Ligustrum texanum – privet
Pittosporum tenuifolium – kohuhu
Pittosporum tenuifolium 'Mrs Gorman' – low growing kohuhu
Plumbago capensis – Cape plumbago
Rhamnus californica 'Eve Case' – coffeeberry

Rhododendron 'Egret' – rhododendron
Rhododendron 'Forsterianum' – rhododendron
Ribes sanguineum 'White Icicle' – white flowering currant
Romneya coulteri – matilija poppy
Spiraea thunbergii – baby's breath spiraea
Ugni molinae – Chilean guava
Viburnum opulus 'Sterile' – snowball tree

Vines

Jasminum mesnyi – primrose jasmine
Kennedia rubicunda – dusky coral pea
Lonicera hildebrandiana – giant Burmese honeysuckle
Rosa banksiae lutea – yellow lady Banks rose
Rosa 'Iceberg' – rose
Wisteria sinensis – Chinese wisteria

Perennials and Grasses

Alstroemeria hybrida 'Marmalade' – Peruvian lily
Bupleurum fruticosum – shrubby hare's ear
Calamagrostis foliosa – leafy reed grass
Campanula muralis – bellflower
Carex divulsa – Berkeley sedge
Ceratostigma griffithii – dwarf plumbago
Eschscholzia californica – California poppy
Festuca californica 'Serpentine Blue' – California fescue
Festuca rubra 'Molate' – Molate red fescue
Geranium x cantabrigiense 'Biokovo' – cranesbill
Helleborus argutifolius – Corsican hellebore
Iris douglasiana 'Canyon Snow' – white Douglas iris
Oxalis oregana – redwood sorrel
Polystichum munitum – Western sword fern
Salvia africana lutea – dune sage
Teucrium scorodonia 'Crispum' – wood sage
Trachelium caeruleum – blue throatwort
Zeugites americana var. Mexicana – zeugites

Water Plants

Alisma plantago-aquatica – mad dog weed
Dichromena colorata – white star grass
Juncus effusus 'Spiralis' – corkscrew rush

LIGHT TOUCH ON THE LAND

Trees

Olea europaea – olive
Pseudotsuga menziesii – Douglas fir
Quercus berberidifolia – scrub oak
Quercus douglasii – blue oak
Quercus kelloggii – black oak

Shrubs

Arctostaphylos 'Emerald Carpet' – carpet manzanita
Arctostahylos bakeri – Baker's manzanita
Arctostaphylos manzanita 'St. Helens' – manzanita
Arctostaphylos 'Pacific Mist' – Pacific mist manzanita
Ceanothus 'Dark Star' – small leaf mountain lilac
Ceanothus foliosus – wavy leaf mountain lilac

Perennials, Grasses and Succulents

Deschampsia cespitosa ssp. cespitosa – tufted hair grass
Mimulus aurantiacus – monkey flower

Dudleya cymosa – canyon liveforever
Iris douglasiana 'Canyon Snow' – white Douglas iris
Muhlenbergia rigens – deer grass
Rhamnus californica – coffeeberry
Salvia sonomensis – creeping sage
Salvia clevelandii 'Winifred Gilman' – Cleveland sage
Sedum spathulifolium 'Cape Blanco' – Pacific stonecrop
Styrax officinalis redivivus – snowdrop bush

Hydroseed Mix

Deschampsia cespitosa ssp. cespitosa – tufted hair grass
Eschscholzia californica – California poppy
Limnanthes douglasii – meadow foam
Nassella pulchra – purple needlegrass
Nemophila menziesii – baby blue eyes

MEADOW PARK

Trees

Acer circinatum – vine maple
Acer griseum – paperbark maple
Corylus americana 'Walt' – hazelnut
Ginkgo biloba – maidenhair tree
Lagerstroemia indica – crape myrtle
Liriodendron tulipifera – tulip tree
Magnolia soulangeana – saucer magnolia
Platanus acerifolia 'Bloodgood' – London plane tree
Pyrus 'Aristocrat' – flowering pear
Quercus coccinea – red oak
Quercus imbricaria – shingle oak
Quercus lobata – valley oak
Quercus rubra – red oak
Salix lasiandra – Pacific willow
Tilia cordata 'Greenspire' – linden
Tilia tomentosa – silver linden

Shrubs & Restios & Vines

Abelia grandiflora – glossy abelia
Aloysia triphylla – lemon verbena
Arctostaphylos 'Emerald Carpet' – manzanita
Arctostaphylos 'Pacific Mist' – manzanita
Arctostaphylos bakeri 'Louis Edmunds' – manzanita
Arctostaphylos manzanita 'Dr. Hurd' – manzanita
Bupleurum fruticosum – shrubby hare's ear
Buxus 'Green Beauty' – boxwood
Buxus 'Winter Gem' – boxwood
Buxus sempervirens – boxwood
Camellia sasanqua 'Setsugekka' – camellia
Ceratostigma griffithii – dwarf plumbago
Cestrum nocturnum – night Jessamine
Chondropetalum elephantinum – cape rush
Coprosma 'Cappuccino' –
Cornus sericea – redtwig dogwood
Corokia cotoneaster – corokia
Corylus cornuta californica – California hazelnut
Cotinus 'Golden Spirit' – smokebush
Daphne odora – winter daphne
Euonymus japonica microphylla – boxleaf euonymus

Gardenia jasminoides 'Veitchii' – gardenia
Gardenia 'White Gem' – dwarf gardenia
Haloragis erecta 'Wellington's Bronze' – toatoa
Hydrangea 'Annabelle' – smooth hydrangea
Hydrangea paniculata 'Limelight' – panicle hydrangea
Hydrangea quercifolia – oakleaf hydrangea
Hydrangea quercifolia 'Sike's Dwarf' – dwarf oakleaf hydrangea
Ilex x 'Wilsonii' – holly
Jasminum officinale grandiflorus – poet's jasmine
Leptospermum horizontalis – horizontal tea tree
Leptospermum laevigatum 'Reevesii' – dwarf tea tree
Phyladelphus coronarius 'Aureus' – golden mock orange
Pittosporum eugenioides – lemonwood
Pittosporum tenuifolium – kohuhu
Pittosporum tobira – tobira
Prunus caroliniana – Carolina cherry
Prunus ilicifolia – holly leaf cherry
Rhamnus California 'Eve Case' – coffeeberry
Rhus typhinia – staghorn sumac
Ribes sanguineum 'White Icicle' – flowering currant
Rosmarinus officinalis 'Ken Taylor' – rosemary
Rubus pentalobus – bramble
Salix purpurea 'Nana' – purple osier
Sambucus caerulea – elderberry
Sarcococca hookeriana humilis – sweet box
Symphoricarpos albus laevigatus – snowberry
Trachelospermum jasminoides – star jasmine
Vaccinium ovatum – huckleberry
Wisteria venusta – silky wisteria
Perennials, Grasses, Ferns, Reed
  Acaena saccaticupula 'Blue Haze' – goose leaf
  Adiantum raddianum – maidenhair fern
  Alchemilla mollis – lady's mantle
  Anigozanthos viridis – kangaroo paw
  Aralia californica – elk clover
  Asparagus 'Myers' – Myers asparagus
  Astilbe 'Bridal Veil' – false spirea
  Campanula 'Dickson's Gold' – bellflower
  Campanula poscharskyana 'Alba' – bellflower
  Carex barbarae – sedge
  Carex divulsa – sedge
  Carex tenuiculmis 'Cappuccino' – sedge
  Carex testacea – sedge
  Centranthus rubber 'Albus' – Jupiter's beard
  Ceranium cantabrigiense 'St Ola' – cranesbil
  Cotula 'Platt's Black' – brass buttons
  Cyrtomium falcatum – hollyleaf fern
  Epimedium versicolor 'Sulphureum' – yellow fairy wings
  Equisetum hyemale robustum – horsetail
  Farfugium japonicum – ligularia
  Gardenia jasminoides 'Veitchii' – gardenia
  Gardenia jasminoides 'White Gem' – gardenia
  Gaura lindheimeri – gaura
  Geranium 'Brookside' – cranesbill
  Geranium 'Nimbus' – cranesbill
  Geranium 'Rozanne' – cranesbill

Geranium himalayense – cranesbill
Geranium x cantabrigiense 'Biokovo' – cranesbill
Hakonechloa macra All Gold – Japanese painted grass
Helleborus argutifolius – Corsican hellebore
Helleborus foetidus – bear's foot hellebore
Hyssopus officinalis – blue form – hyssop
Jarava (Stipa) ichu – feather grass
Knautia macedonica – scabious
Laurentia fluviatilis – blue star creeper
Lavandula x intermedia 'Grosso' – lavender
Luzula sylvatica 'Aurea' – wood rush
Melissa officinalis 'All Gold' – lemon balm
Miscanthus 'Morning Light' – silver maiden grass
Muehlenbeckia astonii – shrubby tororaro
Muehlenbeckia axillaris – dwarf mattress vine
Muehlenbeckia complexa – mattress vine
Muhlenbergia capillaris – pink muhly
Muhlenbergia dumosa – bamboo muhly
Muhlenbergia rigens – deer grass
Origanum laevigatum 'Hopleys' – ornamental oregano
Origanum majorana – marjoram
Pelargonium sidoides – geranium
Pelargonium x fragrans 'Nutmeg' – scented geranium
Pennisetum 'Little Bunny' – dwarf fountain grass
Phygelius 'Snow Queen' – cape fuchsia
Polystichum munitum – western sword fern
Salvia uliginosa – bog sage
Satureja montana – winter savory
Scabiosa atropurpurea 'Black Knight' – pincushion flower
Scabiosa ochroleuca – yellow scabiosa
Tanacetum 'Inca Gold' – tansy
Thymus vulgaris – thyme
Trachelium caeruleum 'Hamer Pandora' – throatwort
Vancouveria hexandra – inside out flower
Verbena bonariensis (patagonica) – verbena
Roses
Noisette
  Rosa 'Crepuscule' – soft orange
  Rosa 'Desprez a Fleur Jaunes' – yellow/peach
Hybrid Tea Roses
  Rosa 'Antique Caramel' – yellow
  Rosa 'Bewitched' – pink
  Rosa 'Brandy' – apricot blend
  Rosa 'Chablis' – white
  Rosa 'Classic Woman' – pink
  Rosa 'Dr. Grill' pink/copper
  Rosa 'Duchesse de Brabant' – pink
  Rosa 'Ebb Tide' – blue/purple
  Rosa 'Emily' – Pink
  Rosa 'Gemini' – pale pink
  Rosa 'Gloire de Dijon' – apricot
  Rosa 'Golden State' – yellow
  Rosa 'Honor' – white
  Rosa 'Julia's Rose' – tan/brown
  Rosa 'Just Joey' – orange
  Rosa 'Lady Hillingdon' – soft yellow

Rosa 'Madame Berkeley' – apricot
Rosa 'Madame Ravary' – pearl/buff
Rosa 'Mc Clinton Tea' – pink
Rosa 'Monsieur Tillier' – orange
Rosa 'Over the Moon' – cream/yellow
Rosa 'Perle d'Or' – apricot
Rosa 'Rubens' – off white
Rosa 'Smoky Vid' – tan
Rosa 'Sombreuil' – white
Rosa 'St Patrick' – green/yellow blend
Rosa 'Strike it Rich' – gold yellow
Rosa 'Summer Dream' – apricot blend
Rosa 'Tantarra ' – soft tan
Austin Roses
  Rosa 'Crown Princess Margartta' – yellow/orange
  Rosa 'Graham Thomas' – yellow
  Rosa 'Jane Austin' – apricot
  Rosa 'Lady Emma Hamilton' – orange/rust
  Rosa 'Pat Austen' – orange
  Rosa 'The Generous gardener' – off white
Romantica Roses
  Rosa 'Abbaye de Cluny' – apricot
  Rosa 'Jean Giono' – yellow blend
  Rosa 'Paul Bocuse' – warm pink
Hybrid Musk Roses
  Rosa 'Felicia' – pink
  Rosa 'Kathleen' – pale pink
  Rosa 'Soleil d'Or' – orange
Floribunda Roses
  Rosa 'Amber Queen' – apricot
  Rosa 'Apricot Nectar' – apricot
  Rosa 'Ginger Snap' – orange
  Rosa 'Margaret Merrill' – white
  Rosa 'Trumpeter' – orange red
  Rosa 'Living Easy' – orange
  Rosa 'Easy Does It' – apricot
  Rosa 'Easy Going' – yellow
Grandiflora Roses
  Rosa 'About Face' – pink
  Rosa 'Honey Dijon' – golden brown
Fruit Trees and Berries
  Apple 'Gala'
  Asian pear – relocated
  Blackberry 'Hull Thornless'
  Blackberry 'Marion'
  Blueberry 'Georgian Gem'
  Blueberry 'O'Neal'
  Blueberry 'Reveille'
  Blueberry 'Sunshine Blue'
  Blueberry 'Top Hat'
  Fig 'Bordeaux'
  Fig 'Flanders'
  Fig 'Osborne Prolific'
  Fig 'Panache Tiger'
  Fig 'White Genoa'
  Hazelnut 'Walt'

Kumquat – relocated
Lemon 'Meyer'
Mulberry relocated
Nectarine 'Double Delight'
Nectarine 'Liz's Late'
Pear 'Comice '
Raspberry 'Indian Summer'
Raspberry 'Willamette Red'
Vitis 'Crimson Seedless'
Vitis 'Himrod Seedless'
Vitis 'Perlette Seedless'
Vitis 'Perlette Seedless'
Vitis 'Ruby Seedless'
Vitis 'Suffolk Red Seedless'
Meadow Seed List
Sun Mix
  Danthonia californica – California oat grass
  Hordeum brachyantherum – meadow barley
  Nassella lepida – foothill needlegrass
Shade Mix
  Danthonia californica – California oat grass
  Festuca rubra – red fescue
  Hordeum brachyantherum – meadow barley
  Melica californica – California melic
  Vulpia microstachys – six weeks fescue

MINIMALIST ROOF DECKS

Shrubs and Vine
  Buxus sempervirens – boxwood
  Corokia cotoneaster – wire netting bush
  Hydrangea quercifolia – oak leaf hydrangea
  Juniperus chinensis 'Torulosa' – Hollywood juniper
  Muehlenbeckia complexa – mattress vine
Perennials
  Haloragis erecta 'Wellington's Bronze' – toatoa
  Oxalis oregana – redwood sorrel
  Pelargonium tomentosum – mint scented geranium

TERRACE CONNECTIONS

Trees
  Cercis canadensis 'Forest Pansy' – Eastern redbud
  Cercis occidentalis – Western redbud
  Cornus nuttallii – Pacific dogwood
  Leptospermum laevigatum – Australian tea tree
  Magnolia stellata 'Royal Star' – star magnolia
  Olea europaea – olive
  Quercus agrifolia – coast live oak
Shrubs and Vines
  Arctostaphylos bakeri 'Louis Edmunds' – Baker's manzanita
  Arctostaphylos 'Pacific Mist' – Pacific mist manzanita
  Arctostaphylos densiflora 'Howard Mc Minn' – vine hill manzanita
  Arctostaphylos manzanita 'Dr. Hurd' – Dr. Hurd manzanita
  Arctostaphylos uva-ursi 'Radiant' – kinnikinnick
  Buxus sempervirens globes – boxwood

Photo by Marion Brenner

Ceanothus 'Concha' – wild lilac
Ceanothus 'Dark Star' – small leaf mountain lilac
Ceanothus 'Ray Hartman' – wild lilac
Ceratostigma griffithii – dwarf plumbago
Clematis cirrhosa – fern leaved clematis
Correa 'Ivory Bells' – wild Australian fuchsia
Daphne odora 'Marginata' – winter daphne
Feijoa sellowiana – pineapple guava
Hydrangea arborescens 'Annabelle' – Annabelle hydrangea
Hydrangea anomala petiolaris – climbing hydrangea
Hydrangea paniculata grandiflora – panicle hydrangea
Hydrangea quercifolia – oak leaf hydrangea
Juniperus chinensis 'Torulosa' – Hollywood juniper
Lonicera sempervirens – red honeysuckle
Olea 'Little Ollie' – dwarf olive
Osmanthus delavayi – Delavay osmanthus
Pittosporum tenuifolium 'Mrs Gorman' – dwarf kohuhu
Prunus caroliniana 'Compacta' – Carolina cherry
Rhododendron 'Forsterianum' – rhododendron
Rhododendron 'Fragrantissimum' – rhododendron
Sarcococca hookeriana humilis – Christmas box
Trachelospermum jasminoides – star jasmine
Vaccinium ovatum – California huckleberry
Wisteria sinensis – Chinese wisteria

Perennials and Ferns
Blechnum spicant – deer fern
Campanula mauritanicus (sabaticus) – ground morning glory
Campanula muralis – wall bellflower
Campanula poscharskyana – Serbian bellflower
Crassula multicava – fairy crassula
Epilobium canum 'Select Mattole' – California fuchsia
Geranium 'Brookside' – cranesbill
Geranium 'Nimbus' – cranesbill
Geranium himalayense – cranesbill
Helleborus argutifolius – Corsican hellebore
Heuchera 'June Bride' – coral bells
Lavandula x intermedia 'Grosso' – lavender
Lavandula x intermedia 'Provence' – French lavender
Pelargonium x fragrans 'Nutmeg' – scented geranium

OAK PARK

Acer circinatum – vine maple
Acer griseum – paperbark maple
Acer japonicum vitifolium – full moon maple
Acer macrophyllum – large leaf maple
Acer palmatum 'Aoyagi' – Japanese maple
Acer palmatum 'Aureum' – Japanese maple
Acer palmatum 'Hogyoku' – Japanese maple
Acer palmatum 'Ichigyoji' – Japanese maple
Acer palmatum 'Katsura' – Japanese maple
Acer palmatum 'Kinran' – Japanese maple
Alnus rhombifolia – white alder
Cornus 'Eddie's White Wonder' – dogwood
Cornus florida relocate – dogwood
Magnolia 'Little Gem' – magnolia

Maytenus boaria – mayten
Salix hindsiana – sandbar willow
Sequoia sempervirens 'Aptos Blue' – redwood

Shrubs & Vines
Abelia grandiflora 'Compacta' – glossy abelia
Aloysia triphylla – lemon verbena
Betula glandulosa – resin birch
Bougainvillea 'Gold Rush' – yellow bougainvillea
Buxus 'Tide Hill' – boxwood
Buxus 'Vardar Valley' – boxwood
Calycanthus occidentalis – western spice bush
Camellia 'Brushfield's Yellow' – camellia
Camellia 'Elegance Champagne' – camellia
Ceratostigma griffithii – dwarf plumbago
Chaenomeles 'Nivalis' – flowering quince
Clematis lasiantha – chaparral clematis
Clematis ligusticifolia – western virgin's bower
Cornus sericea – red osier dogwood
Correa 'Ivory Bells' – Australian fuchsia
Corylus cornuta californica – California hazelnut
Cotinus 'Pink Champagne' – smoke bush
Daphne odora – winter daphne
Euonymus japonicus microphyllus – boxleaf euonymus
Feijoa sellowiana – pineapple guava
Hardenbergia violacea – purple vine lilac
Hydrangea 'Blue Billow' – hydrangea
Hydrangea 'Blue lace cap' – hydrangea
Hydrangea 'Shooting Star' – lacecap hydrangea
Hydrangea anomala petiolaris – climbing hydrangea
Hydrangea arborescens 'Annabelle' – hydrangea
Hydrangea paniculata 'Limelight' – panicle hydrangea
Hydrangea paniculata grandiflora – peegee hydrangea
Hydrangea quercifolia – oakleaf hydrangea
Hydrangea quercifolia 'Sike's Dwarf' – dwarf oakleaf hydrangea
Iochroma cyaneum 'Royal Blue' – violet churur
Jasminum leratii – Leratii jasmine
Loropetalum chinense – fringe flower
Muehlenbeckia complexa – mattress vine
Myrica californica – pacific wax myrtle
Olea europaea 'Little Ollie' – olive shrub
Osmanthus delavayi – Delavay osmanthus
Pieris japonica 'Prelude' – Japanese pieris
Pittosporum tenuifolium 'Silver Magic' – silver magic kohuhu
Pittosporum eugenioides – tarata
Pittosporum tenuifolium – kohuhu
Pittosporum tenuifolium 'Golf Ball' – golf ball kohuhu
Pittosporum tenuifolium 'Kirsti' – kirsti kohuhu
Pittosporum tenuifolium 'Marjorie Channon' – Marjorie Channon kohuhu
Pittosporum tenuifolium 'Mrs Gorman' – Mrs. Gorman kohuhu
Pittosporum tobira – mock orange
Rhamnus californica 'Mound San Bruno' – coffeeberry
Rhamnus californicus 'Eve Case' – coffeeberry
Rhododendron 'Forsterianum' – rhododendron
Salix purpurea 'Nana' – dwarf artic willow
Sambucus canadensis 'Nova' – elderberry

Sambucus canadensis 'York' – elderberry
Sambucus nigra 'Black Beauty' – elderberry
Sarcococca hookeriana humilis – sweet box
Stephanotis floribunda – waxflower
Symphoricarpos rivularis – snowberry
Taxus x media 'Densiformis' – dense yew
Trachelospermum jasminoides – star jasmine
Vaccinium ovatum – huckleberry
Viburnum tinus – laurustinus
Wisteria venusta – silky wisteria

Roses

Rosa 'Buff Beauty'
Rosa 'Cecile Brunner'
Rosa 'Charlotte'
Rosa 'Crème de la Crème
Rosa 'Crocus Rose'
Rosa 'Gloire de Dijon'
Rosa 'Iceberg'–shrub form
Rosa 'Just Joey'
Rosa 'Little White Pet'
Rosa 'Louise Odier'
Rosa 'Madame Isaac Pereire'
Rosa 'Moonlight'
Rosa 'Peachy Creeper'
Rosa 'Reine des Violettes'
Rosa 'Reve d'Or'
Rosa 'Sally Holmes'
Rosa 'Sharifa Asma'
Rosa 'Wise Portia'
Rosa banksia lutea
Rosa eglanteria
Rosa glauca
Rosa pimpinellifolia
Rosa sericea pteracantha

Perennials, Grasses & Ferns

Alchemilla mollis – lady's mantle
Anemona x hybrida 'Honorine Jobert' – Japanese anemone
Angelica gigas – Korean angelica
Anthriscus sylvestris 'Raven's Wing' – Queen Anne's lace
Aquilegia chrysantha – yellow columbine
Aralia californica – elk clover
Aster 'Purple Viking' – michaelmas daisy
Aster cordifolius – blue wood aster
Aster divaricatus – white wood aster
Astrantia major – masterwort
Campanula muralis – bellflower
Campanula poscharskyana – Serbian bellflower
Carex divulsa – Berkeley sedge
Carex nudata – naked sedge
Chasmanthium latifolium – oat grass
Chrysanthemum parthenium 'Aureum' – golden feverfew
Clivia miniata – bush lily
Cyrtomium falcatum – holly fern
Dianthus 'Tiny Rubies' – carnation
Epimedium x versicolor 'Sulphureum' – bishop's hat
Eupatorium 'Gateway' – joe pye weed

Festuca rubra 'Molate' – red fescue
Gaura lindheimeri 'So White' – white gaura
Geranium 'Brookside' – cranesbill
Geranium 'Jolly Bee' – cranesbill
Geranium 'Orion' – cranesbill
Geranium 'Rozanne' – cranesbill
Geranium himalayense – cranesbill
Geranium macrorrhizum 'Album' – cranesbill
Geranium phaeum 'Album' – cranesbill
Geranium x cantabrigiense 'St Ola' – cranesbill
Gypsophila paniculata – baby's breath
Hakonechloa macra 'All Gold' – Japanese painted grass
Helleborus argutifolius – Corsican hellebore
Heracleum lanatum – cow parsley
Heuchera 'June Bride' – white coral bell
Iris douglasiana blue form – Douglas iris
Lavandula stoechas 'Otto Quast' – lavender
Milium effusum 'Aureum' – golden wood millet
Origanum laevigatum 'Hopleys' – Hopleys ornamental oregano
Oxalis oregana – white form – redwood sorrel
Pelargonium 'Apple Cider' – scented geranium
Pelargonium 'Nutmeg' – scented geranium
Pelargonium 'Old Spice' – scented geranium
Pelargonium tomentosum – mint scented geranium
Penstemon 'Blackbird' – beardtongue
Polystichum munitum – western sword fern
Salvia 'Mesa Purple' – purple sage
Salvia 'Purple Majesty' – sage
Salvia azurea grandiflora – blue sage
Salvia leucantha – Mexican sage
Salvia uliginosa – bog sage
Smilacina (Maianthemum) stellata – false Solomon's seal
Tellima grandiflora – fringe cup
Trachelium caeruleum 'Hamer Pandora' – throatwort
Verbena bonariensis (patagonica) – verbena

Bee Salon Plant List

Borago officinalis – borage
Buddleja davidii 'Black Night' – butterfly bush
Ceanothus 'Dark Star' – small leaf mountain lilac
Eriogonum arborescens – buckwheat
Phacelia tanacetifolia – lacy phacelia
Rosmarinus officinalis 'Ken Taylor' – rosemary
Rosmarinus officinalis 'Tuscan Blue' – rosemary
Salix caprea – goat willow
Teucrium chamaedrys – wall germander

Edibles

Allium schoenoprasum – chives
Artemisia dracunculus – tarragon
Cynara scolymus – artichoke
Ficus caryca 'Brown Turkey' – fig
Laurus nobilis – bay leaf
Origanum majorama – marjoram
Origanum vulgare – oregano
Punica granatum – pomegranate
Rosmarinus officinalis – rosemary
Rubus 'Triple Crown' – blackberry

Photo by Marion Brenner

Rubus fruticosus 'Oregon Cutleaf' – blackberry
Rubus idaeus 'Amity' – raspberry
Rubus idaeus 'Dorman Red' – raspberry
Rubus idaeus 'Fall Gold' – yellow raspberry
Rubus roribaccus 'Lucretia' – Lucretia dewberry
Salvia officinalis – sage
Satureja montana – winter savory
Thymus 'Lemon' – lemon thyme
Thymus 'Lime' – lime thyme
Thymus x citriodorus 'Argenteus' – silver thyme
Thymus vulgaris – thyme
Ugni molinae – Chilean guava
Vaccinium corymbosum 'Legacy' – blueberry
Vaccinium corymbosum 'Misty' – blueberry
Vaccinium corymbosum 'Sunshine Blue' – blueberry

Hydroseed Mix
Carex brevicaulis – short stem sedge
Melica torreyana – Torrey's melic grass
Montia perfoliata – miner's lettuce
Nassella lepida – foothill needleg

WOODLAND CLEARING

Trees
Cryptomeria japonica – Japanese cryptomeria
Ginkgo biloba – maidenhair tree
Nyssa sylvatica – black tupelo
Quercus agrifolia – coast live oak
Sequoia sempervirens 'Aptos Blue' – redwood
Tilia cordata – little leaf linden

Shrubs & Vines
Abelia grandiflora 'Prostrate White' – glossy abelia
Arctostaphylos 'Pacific Mist' – Pacific Mist manzanita
Buddleja lindleyana – butterfly bush
Camellia sasanqua 'White Doves' – camelia
Ceanothus 'Concha' – wild lilac
Convolvulus cneorum – silverbush
Coprosma kirkii 'Variegata' – creeping mirror plant
Cotinus coggygria – smoke bush
Euonymus japonica microphylla – boxleaf euonymus
Garrya elliptica – silktassel
Hydrangea quercifolia – oak leaf hydrangea
Jasminum officinale 'Grandiflorus' – poet's jasmine
Lantana 'Aloha' – lantana
Olea europaea 'Little Ollie' – olive shrub
Pittosporum tenuifolium – kohuhu
Pittosporum tobira 'Variegata' – mockorange
Polygonum aubertii – silver lace vine
Rhamnus californica 'Mound San Bruno' – coffeeberry
Sarcococca ruscifolia – sweet box
Spiraea vanhouttii – baby's breath spiraea

Roses
Rosa 'Fair Bianca' – rose
Rosa 'Glamis Castle' – rose
Rosa 'Pat Austin' – rose
Rosa 'Shropshire Lad' – rose
Rosa 'Sombreuil' – climbing rose
Rosa 'The Impressionist' – rose
Rosa 'Tropicana' – rose

Perennials, Grasses & Restios
Achillea 'Coronation Gold' – yarrow
Centranthus ruber 'Albus' – Jupiter's beard
Chondropetalum tectorum – cape rush
Erigeron karvinskianus – fleabane
Fargesia nitida – blue fountain bamboo
Festuca glauca 'Elijah's Blue' – blue fescue
Geranium x cantabrigiense 'St Ola' – cranesbill
Lavandula x intermedia 'Provence' – lavender
Limonium perezii – sea holly
Muhlenbergia rigens – deer grass
Penstemon 'Purple Tiger' – beardtongue
Perovskia atriplicifolia – Russian sage
Salvia confertiflora – red sage
Salvia uliginosa – bog sage
Trachelium caeruleum – throatwort
Uncinia uncinata – red hook sedge
Verbena bonariensis (patagonica) – verbena

Fruit Trees
Apple tree – 'Fuji'
Cherry tree – 'Angela'
Cherry tree – 'Bing'
Fig tree – 'Black Mission'
Lemon tree – 'Meyer'
Loquat – 'Champagne'
Mulberry tree – 'Oscar'
Pear tree – 'Fanstil'
Pear tree – 'Rescue'
Plum tree – 'Golden Nectar'
Pomegranate – 'Wonderful'
Quince – 'Smyrna'

Edibles
Allium schoenoprasum – Chives
Aloysia triphylla – Lemon verbena
Origanum majorana – Marjoram
Origanum vulgare – Oregano
Petroselinum sp. – Parsley
Rosmarinus officinalis – Rosemary
Artemisia dracunculus – Tarragon
Thymus vulgaris – Thyme

OPEN RANGE

Trees
Acer macrophyllum – large leaf maple
Ginkgo biloba – maidenhair tree
Lagerstroemia indica white – crape myrtle
Platanus acerifolia 'Bloodgood' – London plane tree
Pyrus 'Aristocrat' – flowering pear
Quercus agrifolia – coast live oak
Tilia cordata – little leaf linden

Shrubs and Vines
  Abelia grandiflora 'Compacta' – glossy abelia
  Arctostaphylos 'Emerald Carpet' – Emerald Carpet manzanita
  Arctostaphylos 'Pacific Mist' – Pacific mist manzanita
  Arctostaphylos bakeri 'Louis Edmunds' – Baker's manzanita
  Arctostaphylos manzanita 'Dr. Hurd' – Dr. Hurd manzanita
  Baccharis pilularis 'Pigeon Point' – coyote bush
  Buxus sempervirens – boxwood
  Calliandra eriophylla – fairy duster
  Ceanothus 'Dark Star' – small leaf mountain lilac
  Ceratostigma griffithii – dwarf plumbago
  Chaenomeles japonica white form – flowering quince
  Cotinus 'Golden Spirit' – smoke bush
  Euonymus japonica microphylla – Japanese euonymus
  Feijoa sellowiana – pineapple guava
  Fremontodendron californicum – flannel bush
  Gardenia jasminoides 'Veitchii' – gardenia
  Gardenia jasminoides 'White Gem' – gardenia
  Garrya elliptica 'James Roof' – silktassel bush
  Hydrangea paniculata grandiflora – panicle hydrangea
  Hydrangea quercifolia – oakleaf hydrangea
  Jasminum officinale 'Fiona Sunrise' – jasmine
  Lavandula x intermedia 'Grosso' – lavender
  Lonicera periclymenum 'Serotina' – honeysuckle
  Olea europaea 'Little Ollie' – dwarf olive
  Osmanthus fragrans – sweet olive
  Pittosporum tenuifolium – kohuhu
  Pittosporum tenuifolium 'Mrs. Gorman' – dwarf kohuhu
  Pittosporum tobira – tobira
  Rhamnus californica 'Mound San Bruno' – coffeeberry
  Ribes sanguineum 'White Icicle' – white flowering currant
  Rosmarinus officinalis 'Ken Taylor' – rosemary
  Teucrium fruticans 'Azureum' – germander
  Vitis x californica 'Roger's Red' – California grape
  Wisteria venusta – white wisteria
Roses
  Rosa 'Apricot Nectar'
  Rosa 'Autumn Delight'
  Rosa 'Cecile Brunner'
  Rosa 'Gertrude Jekyll'
  Rosa 'Golden Celebration'
  Rosa 'Iceberg' shrub form
  Rosa 'Moonstone'
  Rosa 'Reve D'Or'
  Rosa 'Sally Holmes'
  Rosa 'Sea Foam'
  Rosa 'Sombreuil'
  Rosa 'William Shakespeare'
  Rosa banksiae lutea
  Rosa chinensis mutabilis
  Rosa sericea pteracantha
Perennials, Grasses, Ferns, Bulbs and Corms
  Agapanthus 'Henryi' – lily of the Nile
  Anthriscus sylvestris 'Ravenswing' – wild chervil
  Aster cordifolius – blue wood aster
  Festuca californica 'Blue Select' – blue select fescue

  Festuca idahoensis 'Muse Meadow' – muse meadow fescue
  Brodiaea elegans – harvest brodiaea
  Fritillaria biflora – chocolate lily
  Gaura lindheimeri 'So White' – gaura
  Geranium 'Brookside' – cranesbill
  Geranium 'Rozanne' – cranesbill
  Geranium himalayense – cranesbill
  Geranium macrorrhizum 'Album' – cranesbill
  Geranium macrorrhizum 'White Ness' – cranesbill
  Helleborus argutifolius – Corsican hellebore
  Heuchera maxima – coral bells
  Iris douglasiana 'Canyon Snow' – white Douglas iris
  Muehlenbeckia axillaris – dwarf mattress vine
  Muhlenbergia capillaris – pink muhly
  Oenothera 'Woodside White' – evening primrose
  Origanum laevigatum 'Hopleys' – Hopleys ornamental oregano
  Carex flagellifera – sedge
  Carex divulsa – Berkeley sedge
  Penstemon 'Holly's White' – white beard tongue
  Penstemon 'Huntington Pink' – pink beard tongue
  Perovskia atriplicifolia – Russian sage
  Polystichum munitum – Western sword fern
  Salvia clevelandii 'Winifred Gilman' – California blue sage
  Salvia leucantha 'Midnight' – Mexican sage
  Salvia uliginosa – bog sage
  Sisyrinchium bellum – blue–eyed grass
  Tanacetum camphoratum – tansy
  Thymus 'Lime' – lime thyme
  Thymus serpyllum 'Elfin' – elfin thyme
Seed Mix
  Danthonia californica – California oat grass
  Eschscholzia californica – California poppy
  Festuca rubra –red fescue
  Nassella cernua – nodding needlegrass
  Nassella pulchra – purple needlegrass

OCEAN FRAME

Trees
  Cupressus macrocarpa – Monterey cypress
  Lyonothamnus floribundus asplenifolius – Catalina ironwood
  Quercus dumosa – scrub oak
  Sequoia sempervirens – coast redwood
Shrubs and Vines
  Baccharis pilularis consanguinea – coyote bush
  Ceanothus 'Dark Star' – small leaf mountain lilac
  Ceanothus gloriosus porrectus – Mt. Vision ceanothus
  Ceanothus griseus horizontalis 'Carmel Creeper' – Carmel creeper ceanothus
  Ceanothus rigidus 'Snowball' – white Monterey lilac
  Ceanothus thyrsiflorus – blueblossom ceanothus
  Ceanothus thyrsiflorus 'Snow Flurry' – white blueblossom ceanothus
  Convolvulus cneorum – bush morning glory
  Leptospermum horizontalis – horizontal tea shrub
  Leptospermum laevigatum – tea tree
  Pittosporum crassifolium 'Compacta' – dwarf karo

Pittosporum tobira – Japanese mockorange
Rhamnus californica – coffeeberry
Rhamnus californica 'Eve Case' – Eve Case coffeeberry
Romneya coulteri – matilija poppy
Rosa 'Fair Bianca' – rose
Salix purpurea 'Nana' – dwarf arctic willow
Salvia leucantha – Mexican sage
Salvia leucophylla 'Point Sal Spreader' – Point Sal purple sage
Solanum jasminoides – potato vine
Spiraea bumalda 'Anthony Waterer' – Bumald spiraea
Tibouchina urvilleana – princess flower
Vaccinium ovatum – California huckleberry

Perennials and Grasses
Epilobium canum – California fuchsia
Eriogonum parvifolium – dune buckwheat
Geranium x cantabrigiense 'Biokovo' – cranesbill
Lavandula x intermedia 'Grosso' – lavender
Limonium perezii – sea lavender
Mimulus aurantiacus – monkey flower
Muhlenbergia rigens – deer grass
Origanum laevigatum 'Hopleys' – Hopley's purple oregano
Pelargonium sidoides – South African geranium
Pelargonium tomentosum – mint scented geranium
Pennisetum setaceum 'Rubrum' – purple fountain grass
Penstemon 'Hidcote Pink' – beard tongue
Perovskia atriplicifolia – Russian sage
Polystichum munitum – western sword fern
Salvia leucantha – Mexican sage

Heather Garden
Calluna vulgaris 'Anthony Davis' – Scotch heather
Calluna vulgaris 'H.E. Beale' – Scotch heather
Calluna vulgaris 'Silver Knight' – Scotch heather
Erica darleyensis 'Alba ' – white heather
Erica darleyensis 'Darley Dale' – pink heather
Erica vagans 'Alba' – white Cornish heath
Daboecia cantabrica 'Alba Globosa' – white Irish heath

Hydroseed Mix
Aquilegia formosa – western columbine
Bromus carinatus – brome
Eschscholzia californica – California poppy
Festuca rubra – red fescue
Lupinus littoralis – seashore lupine
Melica imperfecta – melic

APPENDIX

Firm Profile

Blasen Landscape Architecture listens attentively for clients' thoughts on how they might most wish to live on their land and builds gardens that provide a pristine and deeply felt encounter with it. Interested in the psychological and aesthetic qualities of land, they work, essentially, to increase their clients' happiness. They start with their dreams, and the land as it is: its natural or constructed shape, the qualities of its breezes, and the plants that are thriving there.

The gardens in this book are growing on the shores of the Pacific Ocean, in the valleys of the California coastal hills, in tight urban lots, and on spacious residential estates. Each is of a sophisticated and seamless high quality and demonstrates Eric Blasen and Silvina Martierena Blasens' ability to intensely intuit and beautifully forge a relevant, contemporary dynamic between architecture and land. Whether a wildflower meadow or a courtyard around a fireplace, the spaces are built sustainably and shine with a single quality: ease with the outdoors. These gardens help their owners live everyday in relationship to the land.

Eric Blasen

Eric Blasen, ASLA, studied art history at the University of London, England, received his Bachelor of Science in Geography from Oregon State University and his Masters of Landscape Architecture from University of Massachusetts, Amherst. He first explored practical design by making furniture and won his first design award for it. In 1993, he cofounded, with his wife, Silvina, Blasen Landscape Architecture, a design studio, in San Anselmo, California. The design team has created landscapes for places of worship, schools, corporate offices, and wineries, but its main focus is large residential gardens, for which it has garnered top American landscape architecture awards. Eric Blasen has taught in the Architecture Department at California College of the Arts, San Francisco, California, and served on many academic juries.

Silvina Martierena Blasen

Silvina Martierena Blasen is a principal of Blasen Landscape Architecture and its plant expert and green practices advocate. After gaining her Certificate in Horticulture from Sierra College, Rocklin, California she became a partner with Stienstra/Martierena Landscape Architecture-Design Build Garden Company in Buenos Aires, Argentina, and nursery manager at Smith & Hawken's original store, in Mill Valley, California. Her passion for planting design and knowledge of the environment result in work that is acclaimed for its creativity and commitment to sustainability.

Project Credits

Urban Play   SAN FRANCISCO, CALIFORNIA
Architect: Gemmill Design
Interior Designer: Mark Cunningham Design, Inc.
General Contractor: Creative Spaces
Lighting Designer: Bouyea & Associates, Inc.

Beach Headlands   STINSON BEACH, CALIFORNIA
Architect: Pfau Long Architecture
General Contractor: Woodworking West, Inc.

Oak Weave   CALIFORNIA
Architect: Jim Jennings Architecture
General Contractor: Webcor Builders
Lighting Designer: Dan Dobt

Light Touch on the Land   CALISTOGA, CALIFORNIA
Architect: Eliot Lee with Steven Harris Architects
and Eun Sun Chun
General Contractor: Beaman Construction

Meadow Park   CALIFORNIA
Architect: Atelier Ugo Sap
Interior Designer: Douglas Durkin Design, Inc.
General Contractor: Van Acker Construction, Inc.
Lighting Designer: Truax Design Group, Inc.
Meadow Consultant: Pacific Open Space, Dave Kaplow

Garden Above   SAN FRANCISCO, CALIFORNIA
Architect: Pfau Long Architecture and David Yama
General Contractor: Matarozzi/Pelsinger, Inc.

Terrace Connections   OAKLAND, CALIFORNIA
Architect: Regan Bice Architects
and Fischer Architecture
Interior Designer: Mobley Bloomfield Design
General Contractor: Ryan Associates
Lighting Designer: TechLinea

Oak Park   CALIFORNIA
Architect: Atelier Ugo Sap

Woodland Clearing ATHERTON, CALIFORNIA
Architect: Aidlin Darling Design
Interior Designer: Suzanne Miller
General Contractor: Plemons Construction
Lighting Designer: Revolver Design

Open Range HEALDSBURG, CALIFORNIA
Architect: Atelier Ugo Sap
Interior Designer: G2 Design
General Contractor: Van Acker Construction, Inc.

Ocean Frame BIG SUR, CALIFORNIA
Architect: Sagan Piechota Architecture
General Contractor: The Kronlund Company
Stone Mason: Edwin Hamilton Stoneworks

Publications and Awards

Books

Designing the Sustainable Site,
ISBN 978-0-470-90009-3. John Wiley & Sons, Inc., 2012

1000 x Landscape Architecture,
ISBN 978-3-938780-60-2. Verlagshaus Braun, 1st edition 2009

New Garden Design: Inspiring Private Paradises,
Zahid Sardar, ISBN 978-1-4236-0334-4, Gibbs Smith, 2008

Magazines

Architectural Digest Magazine, "Point of View," February 2011
Dwell Magazine, "Good Clean Fun," July/August 2011
Landscape Architecture Magazine, "Let the Good Times Climb, Slide, & Roll," February 2011
Garden Design Magazine, "Stand & Deliver," October 2009
Landscape Architecture Magazine, "Lee Landscape," August 2009
BBC Gardens Illustrated Magazine, "California Dreaming," March 2009
New York Times, "In Harmony with Earth, Wind and Fire," January 1, 2009
Garden Design Magazine, "D-e--cor: Selective Focus," March 2007
House and Garden Magazine, "Silvina and Eric Blasen, The Naturalists," April 2006
San Francisco Magazine, "A Fresh Take on Vintage," February 2006
Metropolitan Home, "Movin' up to Modern," October 2005
San Francisco Chronicle Magazine, "Camp Stinson," August 2005

Western Interiors and Design, "Beach Breeze," May/June 2005
Dwell Magazine, "Pfau Play in the Presidio," June 2003
San Francisco Chronicle, "Garage Startup," May 11, 2003
Gardens Illustrated Magazine, Breaking Ground, September 2002
One Magazine, In the Flow, February 2001
Landscape Architecture Magazine, "Beyond Terracotta," December 1996
San Francisco Chronicle, "Isn't It Romantic," February 14, 1996
Image Magazine, San Francisco Examiner, "Turning the Tables," June 20, 1995
San Francisco Examiner Magazine, "Revive, Renew, Relive," April 2, 1995
San Francisco Examiner Magazine, "Cutting Edges," January 15, 1995

Awards & Recognitions

Green Good Design 2012 Urban Design Planning/Landscape Architecture Category
ASLA Professional Awards 2010 Residential Design Category, Honor Award
ASLA/NCC Professional Awards 2010 Merit Award
ASLA Professional Awards 2009 Residential Design Category, Honor Award
Garden Design Magazine, 2009 Green Awards Winner
ASLA/NCC Professional Awards 2008 Honor Award
2005 California Council AIA award for MOCA @ LBC
2003 California Council AIA award for CCA/Clifton Hall
2003 San Francisco AIA; Excellence in Design award for CCA/Clifton Hall
AIA East Bay 1995 Firestorm Design Awards; Excellence in Residential Design, KAYO Garden
San Francisco Landscape Garden Show 1993 Honor Awards

Book Credits

Hazel White

Hazel White is the author of eleven books on gardening and landscape design; her writing has also appeared in national and international magazines, including the *San Francisco Chronicle* magazine, *Garden Design,* BBC *Gardens Illustrated*, the *London Telegraph* magazine, and *Haüser*. She is a published poet and in 2008 was one of the winners of a monologue competition at San Francisco Museum of Modern Art. She lives in San Francisco.

Catherine Wagner

Catherine Wagner is an international artist, working photographically and in site-specific public art, and lecturer. She has received many major awards, including a Guggenheim Fellowship, NEA Fellowships, and the Ferguson Award. In 2001, Wagner was named one of *Time Magazine's* Fine Arts Innovators of the Year. Her work is represented in major collections around the world. She lives in the San Francisco Bay Area.

Marion Brenner

Marion Brenner's photographs of landscape architecture and gardens have appeared in numerous books and magazines, including *House & Garden, Martha Stewart Living, House Beautiful, The New York Times,* and *Elle Décor*. Her photography is also in the Bancroft Library Collection at University of California Berkeley and in the permanent collections of the San Francisco Museum of Modern Art and the Berkeley Art Museum. She lives in Berkeley, California.

Pablo Mandel

Pablo Mandel is an art director and book designer based in Vancouver, Canada, and Buenos Aires, Argentina. His book designs have been published worldwide and won several awards, including the Canadian Society of Landscape Architects' National Merit Award 2011 for *Grounded*, and the Bookbuilders West's Certificate of Excellence (Image-driven trade books, 2009, 2010, 2011). Pablo graduated from Buenos Aires University in 1995 with a degree in Graphic Design, and he is a Certified Member of the Society of Graphic Designers of Canada.

Acknowledgements

We would like to thank our clients for their support and encouragement. Marion Brenner for such wonderful photography that tell the visual story of our gardens. Also Hazel White for her thoughtful and poetic writings for this book. Our dear friend Catherine Wagner for her critical contributions to our work. Gordon Goff at ORO *editions* for sharing this work with a much larger audience. Pablo Mandel for his beautiful layout and design. Ann Bartram Young for sharing her California native plants knowledge. Kristin Jakob for reviewing the spelling of our plant lists. All the architects, interior designers with whom we worked with on these projects, for being such good collaborators, and the good contractors and craftsmen for their attention to detail and for caring. We also want to thank Joshua Aidlin, Andrea Cockran, Mona El Khafif, Peter Pfau and Ugo Sap for their endorsements.

We are deeply thankful to the very talented design team at our office, Gary Rasmussen, Hsiaochien Chuang, Beth Lee, and Nate Dunham without whom the work in this book would not have been possible.

—Eric Blasen & Silvina Martierena Blasen

Photo by JD Peterson